Federal Financial Institutions Examination Council

ANNUAL REPORT 2012

Board of Governors of the Federal Reserve System, Consumer Financial Protection Bureau, Federal Deposit Insurance Corporation, National Credit Union Administration, Office of the Comptroller of the Currency, State Liaison Committee

Federal Financial Institutions Examination Council

ANNUAL REPORT 2012

Board of Governors of the Federal Reserve System, Consumer Financial Protection Bureau, Federal Deposit Insurance Corporation, National Credit Union Administration, Office of the Comptroller of the Currency, State Liaison Committee

MEMBERS OF THE COUNCIL

John Munn, Director, Nebraska Department of Banking & Finance; Richard Cordray, Director, Consumer Financial Protection Bureau; Debbie Matz, FFIEC Chairman, Chairman, National Credit Union Administration; Daniel K. Tarullo, Member, Board of Governors of the Federal Reserve System; Thomas Curry, FFIEC Vice Chairman, Comptroller of the Currency, Office of the Comptroller of the Currency; Martin J. Gruenberg, Chairman, Federal Deposit Insurance Corporation.

LETTER OF TRANSMITTAL

Federal Financial Institutions
   Examination Council
Arlington, VA 22226
March 29, 2013

The President of the Senate
The Speaker of the House of Representatives

Pursuant to the provisions of section 1006(f) of the Financial Institutions Regulatory and Interest Rate Control Act of 1978 (12 U.S.C. § 3305), I am pleased to submit the 2012 Annual Report of the Federal Financial Institutions Examination Council.

Respectfully,

Debbie Matz
Chairman

TABLE OF CONTENTS

Message from the Chairman

FFIEC Chairman Debbie Matz

I am honored to have served as the Chairman of the Federal Financial Institutions Examination Council for the past two years. Over this time, the Council emphasized cooperative and collaborative approaches to promote uniformity in the supervision of financial institutions as appropriate. We made progress in providing the financial industry necessary guidance, raising the visibility of the Appraisal Subcommittee in light of its new statutory responsibilities, and increasing state-of-the-art training to examiners.

The Council, through our task forces, released significant guidance communications highlighting risk areas, including Interest Rate Risk and Outsourced Cloud Computing. Our follow-up to the January 2010 Interest Rate Risk Management Advisory provided additional guidance regarding risk mitigation expectations and practices. Our Statement on Outsourced Cloud Computing highlighted key risk considerations, particularly the importance of due diligence when implementing this technology service model. Our proposed Social Media Guidance discussed consumer protection and compliance laws and their applicability to activities conducted through social media. These Council issuances support our mission of promoting consistent supervision of financial institutions.

With renewed focus and additional responsibilities assigned to the Appraisal Subcommittee (ASC) by the Dodd-Frank Wall Street Reform and Consumer Protection Act, the member-agency principals designated higher-level, senior staff members to serve on the ASC Board. With the ASC Board's high-level strategic guidance, the ASC made progress in developing a phased approach to implement the appraisal complaint hotline and website and drafting updated proposed policy statements. Efforts continue to finalize preparations for the appraisal complaint hotline opening in March 2013.

The Council provided 95 sessions of courses and conferences through the Task Force on Examiner Education and the FFIEC Examiner Education Office. Almost 3,500 federal regulatory and state supervisory agency staff received superior training on many industry-specific topics. A specialized FFIEC course focusing on significant consumer compliance issues was developed in 2012, and two Consumer Compliance Specialists Conferences are scheduled in 2013.

The Council continues to fulfill our mission of promoting uniformity of supervision, where feasible, throughout the financial industry. In addition, through guidance and staff training, we identified emerging risks providing institutions the opportunity to avoid or mitigate their adverse consequences.

I appreciate the opportunity to have led this distinguished Council and look forward to continue working with my colleagues to advance future FFIEC initiatives.

OVERVIEW OF THE FEDERAL FINANCIAL INSTITUTIONS EXAMINATION COUNCIL OPERATIONS

The Federal Financial Institutions Examination Council (FFIEC or Council) was established on March 10, 1979, pursuant to title X of the Financial Institutions Regulatory and Interest Rate Control Act of 1978 (FIRIRCA), Public Law 95-630. The purpose of title X, cited as the Federal Financial Institutions Examination Council Act of 1978, was to create a formal interagency body empowered to prescribe uniform principles, standards, and report forms for the federal examination of financial institutions by the Board of Governors of the Federal Reserve System (FRB), the Federal Deposit Insurance Corporation (FDIC), the National Credit Union Administration (NCUA), and the Office of the Comptroller of the Currency (OCC) and to make recommendations to promote uniformity in the supervision of financial institutions. To encourage the application of uniform examination principles and standards by the state and federal supervisory authorities, the Council established, in accordance with the requirement of FIRIRCA, an advisory State Liaison Committee (SLC). In accordance with the Financial Services Regulatory Relief Act of 2006, the Chair of the SLC was added as a voting member of the Council in October 2006. In accordance with the Dodd-Frank Wall Street Reform and Consumer Protection Act of 2010 (Dodd-Frank Act), the Director of the Consumer Financial Protection Bureau (CFPB) was added as a voting member of the Council in July 2011, replacing the Director of the former Office of Thrift Supervision.

The Council is responsible for developing uniform reporting systems for federally supervised financial institutions, their holding companies, and the nonfinancial institution subsidiaries of those institutions and holding companies. It conducts schools for examiners employed by the five federal member agencies represented on the Council and makes those schools available to employees of state agencies that supervise financial institutions.

The Council was given additional statutory responsibilities by section 340 of the Housing and Community Development Act of 1980, Public Law 96-399. Among these responsibilities are the implementation of a system to facilitate public access to data that depository institutions must disclose under the Home Mortgage Disclosure Act of 1975 (HMDA) and the aggregation of annual HMDA data, by census tract, for each metropolitan statistical area.

Title XI of the Financial Institutions Reform, Recovery, and Enforcement Act of 1989 established the Appraisal Subcommittee within the Council. The functions of the subcommittee are (1) monitoring the requirements, including a code of professional responsibility, established by states for the certification and licensing of individuals who are qualified to perform appraisals in connection with federally related transactions; (2) monitoring the appraisal standards established by the federal financial institution regulatory agencies and the former Resolution Trust Corporation; (3) maintaining a national registry of appraisers who are certified and licensed by a state, and are also eligible to perform appraisals in federally related transactions; and (4) monitoring the practices, procedures, activities, and organizational structure of the Appraisal Foundation, a nonprofit educational corporation established by the U.S. appraisal industry.

The Secure and Fair Enforcement for Mortgage Lending Act of 2008 (SAFE Act), enacted as title V of the Housing and Economic Recovery Act of 2008, established the responsibility for the federal financial institution regulatory agencies, through the FFIEC and in conjunction with the Farm Credit Administration (FCA), to develop and maintain a system for registering employees of depository institutions and certain of their subsidiaries' loan originators with the Nationwide Mortgage Licensing System and Registry (NMLSR). The SAFE Act and implementing regulations require certain information about loan originators to be furnished to the NMLSR concerning an employee's identity, including (A) fingerprints for submission to the Federal Bureau of Investigation and any governmental agency or entity authorized to receive such information for a state and national criminal history background check and (B) personal history and experience, including authorization for the NMLSR to obtain information related to any administrative, civil, or criminal findings by any governmental jurisdiction. On July 21, 2011, pursuant to the Dodd-Frank Act, the authority for rulemaking and authority to develop and maintain the NMLSR generally was transferred to the CFPB.

Members of the Council

The Council has six members, and in 2012 it was comprised of

- a member of the FRB, appointed by the Chairman of the Board;

- the Chairman of the FDIC;

- the Chairman of the NCUA;

- the Comptroller of the Currency;

- the Director of the CFPB; and

- the Chairman of the SLC.

Six staff task forces effectively administer the full spectrum of projects in the Council's functional areas, including but not limited to researching future enhancements for reporting, examiner training products, and examiner guidance. The task forces are each comprised of six senior officials, drawn from the five federal member agencies, and a representative of the SLC. Each is tasked with one of the following subject matters:

- Consumer Compliance

- Examiner Education

- Information Sharing

- Reports

- Supervision

- Surveillance Systems

The Council has a Legal Advisory Group (LAG), composed of the general or chief counsel of each member entity, to provide support to the Council and staff in the substantive areas of concern. The task forces and the LAG provide research and develop analytical papers and proposals on the issues that the Council addresses. In addition, the Council also has an Agency Liaison Group, comprised of senior officials responsible for coordinating the FFIEC work of their respective agencies' staff members.

Administration of the Council

The Council holds regular meetings at least twice a year. Other Council meetings may be convened whenever called by the Chairman or four or more Council members. The Council's activities are funded in several ways. Most of the Council's funds are derived from assessments on its five federal member agencies. It receives tuition fees from non-agency attendees to cover some of the costs associated with its examiner education program.

In 2012, the FRB continued to provide budget and accounting services to the Council. The Council is supported by a small, full-time administrative staff in its operations office and in its examiner education program, which are located at the FDIC's L. William Seidman Center in Arlington, Virginia. Each Council staff member is detailed (some permanently) from one of the five federal member agencies represented on the Council.

RECORD OF COUNCIL ACTIVITIES

The Federal Financial Institutions Examination Council in session.

The following section is a chronological record of the official actions taken by the FFIEC during 2012, pursuant to the Federal Financial Institutions Examination Council Act of 1978, as amended, and the Home Mortgage Disclosure Act of 1975 (HMDA), as amended.

January 26, 2012

Action. Approved the Central Data Repository (CDR) Steering Committee's Task Order #8.

Explanation. The Council is required to approve task orders that exceed a specific dollar amount. Task Order #8 covers funds for CDR enhancements to (1) improve the National Information Center's CDR structure and the Uniform Bank Performance Report (UBPR) pages, (2) add an online UBPR User's Guide, (3) cover UBPR Bulk Downloads, (4) modify calculations on the Micro Data Reference Manual start dates, and (5) provide a data patch to correct derived March 2008 Call

Report data. Task Order #8 also includes a reallocation of funds within the budget and a setting aside of funds for a bonus payment to the contractor should performance goals be met.

January 26, 2012

Action. Approved the CDR Steering Committee's Task Order #9.

Explanation. The Council is required to approve task orders that exceed a specific dollar amount. Task Order #9 covers funds for CDR enhancements to support the functionality request by the FDIC's Examination Tools Suite (ETS) program, which includes new web service methods to provide information required to create UBPR pages with the ETS application.

February 1, 2012

Action. Approved the issuance of the Council's annual interagency awards.

Explanation. The Council has an interagency awards program that recognizes individuals of the member agencies who have provided outstanding service to the Council on interagency projects and programs during the previous year.

February 27, 2012

Action. Approved selection of the Appraisal Subcommittee Chair, Peter W. Gillispie, U.S. Department of Housing and Urban Development.

Explanation. The Council is required to approve the selection of the Appraisal Subcommittee Chair, who serves a two-year term.

February 27, 2012

Action. Approved the appointment of six task force chairs.

Explanation. The chairs for all six standing task forces are approved annually and are drawn from management and staff of the five federal member agencies and representatives of the State Liaison Committee (SLC).

March 8, 2012

Action. Approved the 2011 annual report of the Council to the Congress.

Explanation. The legislation establishing the Council requires that, not later than April 1 of each year, the Council publish an annual report covering its activities during the preceding year.

March 19, 2012

Action. Approved re-appointment of SLC member, David Cotney, Massachusetts Division of Banks Commissioner.

Explanation. The Council appoints two of the SLC members. The remaining three members are designated by the Conference of State Banking Supervisors, the American Council of State Savings Supervisors, and the National Association of State Credit Union Supervisors.

October 31, 2012

Action. Approved CDR Contract Re-Compete Process, naming the FDIC to serve as the procurement agent.

Explanation. The current CDR contract for system support to process the Consolidated Reports of Condition and Income (Call Report) and the UBPR will expire in November 2013. An interagency team identified and analyzed alternatives for continuing system support beyond November 2013, and a case recommending one of the alternatives was presented to the Council for consideration.

December 3, 2012

Action. Approved the 2013 Council budget.

Explanation. The Council is required to approve the annual budget that funds the Council's staff, programs, and activities.

STATE LIAISON REPORT

State Liaison Committee (from the left to right): David Cotney (MA), Douglas Foster (TX), Chairman John Munn (NE), Charles A. Vice (KY), and Harold E. Feeney (TX).

The State Liaison Committee (SLC) consists of five representatives from state regulatory agencies that supervise financial institutions. The representatives are appointed for two-year terms.

An SLC member may have his or her two-year term extended by the appointing organization for an additional, consecutive two-year term. Each year, the SLC elects one of its members to serve as chairman for 12 months. The Council elects two of the five members of the SLC. The American Council of State Savings Supervisors, the Conference of State Bank Supervisors (CSBS), and the National Association of State Credit Union Supervisors designate the other three members. The members of the SLC serve as an important conduit to their state colleagues and represent state supervisory interests before the Council.

The SLC is represented on the Council's task forces and working groups by state supervisors from around the country. The CSBS provides staff support to the SLC representatives and serves as the primary liaison to the Federal Financial Institutions Examination Council (FFIEC) staff for all administrative matters.

In connection with its role on the Council, the SLC meets in person before each Council meeting to review the agenda and discuss topics of interest which may come before the Council. The SLC welcomes leadership and policymakers from the FFIEC member agencies to meet with them during these briefings to engage in informal dialogue. Those who participated this year included Thomas Curry, Comptroller of the Currency, Office of the Comptroller of the Currency; Richard Cordray, Director, Consumer Financial Protection Bureau (CFPB); Steven Antonakes, Associate Director, Division of Supervision-Enforcement & Fair Lending, CFPB; Paul Sanford, Acting Chief of Staff, Division of Supervision-Enforcement & Fair Lending, CFPB; and Judith Dupre, Executive Secretary, FFIEC.

ACTIVITIES OF THE INTERAGENCY STAFF TASK FORCES

Task Force on Consumer Compliance

The Task Force on Consumer Compliance promotes policy coordination, a common supervisory approach, and uniform enforcement of consumer protection laws and regulations. The task force identifies and analyzes emerging consumer compliance issues and develops proposed policies and procedures to foster consistency among the agencies. Additionally, the task force reviews legislation, regulations, and policies at the state and federal level that may have a bearing on the compliance responsibilities of the member agencies.

During 2012, the task force relied on the Home Mortgage Disclosure Act (HMDA)/Community Reinvestment Act (CRA) Data Collection Subcommittee and several ad hoc working groups to carry out its mission. The task force meets monthly to address and resolve common issues in compliance supervision. While significant issues or recommendations are referred to the Council for action, the Council has delegated to the task force the authority to make certain decisions and recommendations.

Initiatives Addressed in 2012

Social Media Guidance

The task force formed a working group to draft guidance on consumer compliance issues related to social media, culminating in the approval of the Social Media Guidance at the September 10, 2012, task force meeting. The individual

Task Force on Consumer Compliance meeting.

agency approval process is under way, after which the Guidance will be published in the *Federal Register* for a 60-day comment period in January 2013 before finalization by the agencies after their consideration of comments. The working group collaborated with the Information Technology Subcommittee of the Task Force on Supervision on specifics within the Guidance.

HMDA/CRA Data Collection Subcommittee Activities

The 2010 census data were released in June 2012. The CRA and HMDA data were processed and aggregated, and were released to the public on September 18, 2012, through the FFIEC website, http://www.ffiec.gov/press/pr091812.htm.

Additionally, the 2013 budget for HMDA and CRA data processing was approved by the task force during its September 10, 2012, meeting and was part of the overall budget package approved by the Council at its December 3, 2012, meeting.

Consumer Compliance Specialists Conference

In 2012, the task force collaborated with the Task Force on Examiner Education and the FFIEC Examiner Education Office to develop and plan the Consumer Compliance Specialists Conference. The conference addresses supervisory updates and emerging issues for experienced examiners. The program was originally planned for October 2012, but was rescheduled for January 2013 due to Hurricane Sandy and will be offered again in October 2013.

Fair Credit Reporting Act (FCRA) Examination Procedures

In March 2012, the task force approved FCRA examination procedures that reflect changes contained in the Dodd-Frank Act. The act amended the FCRA to require the disclosure on FCRA adverse action notices of a credit score that is used in taking any adverse action based "in whole or in part on any information in a consumer report." In addition, the exam procedures incorporated Dodd-Frank Act changes to the FCRA's

implementing regulation on risk-based pricing notices.

Regulation Z (Truth in Lending Act) Examination Proceduress

On July 12, 2012, the task force approved updates to examination procedures related to Regulation Z. Primarily, these updates were technical changes required as a result of the Dodd-Frank Act, such as changes to the numbering of sections and the relocation of various footnotes.

Substantive changes to the limitations on fees charged prior to the opening of an account, as well as corrections to the civil liability provisions and the open-end annual percentage rate calculation were also incorporated and approved.

Consumer Compliance Specialists Conference Speakers:

Left: Debbie Matz, FFIEC Chairman, Chairman, National Credit Union Administration and Richard Cordray, Director, Consumer Financial Protection Bureau.

Below: Thomas Curry, FFIEC Vice Chairman, Comptroller of the Currency, Office of the Comptroller of the Currency.

Remittance Transfer Rule Examination Procedures

The task force formed a working group to develop examination procedures to assess compliance with the new remittance rule issued pursuant to section 1073 of the Dodd-Frank Act, which amends Regulation E, which implements the Electronic Fund Transfer Act. The procedures will be issued before the rule goes into effect.

Garnishment Rule Examination Procedures

The task force has formed a working group to develop examination procedures that will be used by the agencies to evaluate depository institutions' compliance with the garnishment rule issued by the Treasury Department and federal benefits agencies. When finalized, the Treasury Department rule will require financial institutions to take steps to alleviate the hardship experienced by account holders who receive certain types of federal benefits when the garnishment process occurs.

Task Force on Examiner Education

The Task Force on Examiner Education oversees the FFIEC's examiner education program on behalf of the Council. The task force promotes interagency education through timely, cost-efficient, state-of-the-art training programs for federal and state examiners and agency staff. The task force develops programs on its own initiative and in response to requests from the Council, Council task forces, and suggestions brought forth by Examiner Education Office (EEO) staff. The EEO also maintains development groups which have been established to provide ongoing content guidance for classes and conferences. Development group members consist of subject matter experts (SMEs) from each FFIEC member entity designated by their task force members. Development group members help the EEO ensure that the course content is relevant, current, and meeting the agencies' training needs.

Each fall, EEO staff prepares a training calendar based on demand from the FFIEC member agencies and state financial institution regulators, which is then approved by the task force. The EEO staff schedules, delivers, and evaluates training programs throughout the year.

Initiatives Addressed in 2012

The task force has continued to ensure that the FFIEC's educational programs meet the needs of agency personnel, are cost–effective, and are widely available. The task force meets monthly with the EEO staff to discuss emerging

2012 FFIEC Training by Agency and Sponsored—Actual, as of December 31, 2012

Event Name	FRB	FRB State Sponsored	FDIC	FDIC State Sponsored	NCUA	OCC	CFPB	FCA	FHFA	Other	Total
Advanced BSA/AML Conference	31	14	32	12	3	28	3	0	0	8	131
Advanced Cash Flow Concepts & Analysis: Beyond	42	10	53	0	7	39	0	3	0	1	155
Advanced Commercial Credit Analysis	16	9	33	13	3	27	0	5	0	0	106
Advanced Fraud Investigation Techniques for Examiners	7	4	7	0	4	5	0	0	1	0	28
Anti-Money Laundering Workshop	13	10	38	11	5	0	2	0	0	2	81
Asset Management Forum	27	7	42	14	0	14	0	0	0	0	104
Capital Markets Conference	42	26	59	14	12	19	2	7	9	0	190
Capital Markets Specialists Conference	36	14	90	4	2	14	1	13	6	2	182
Cash Flow Construction and Analysis	42	17	88	13	13	46	0	2	0	0	221
Commercial Real Estate	57	17	180	54	22	48	0	0	3	1	382
Community Financial Institutions Lending Forum	20	10	35	7	6	18	0	2	0	0	98
Consumer Compliance Specialists Conference	0	0	0	0	0	0	0	0	0	0	0
Distressed Commercial Real Estate Analysis	30	17	160	33	12	29	0	0	1	2	284
Financial Crimes Seminar	24	16	177	7	18	30	0	2	2	4	280
Fraud Identification On-line Training	1	0	23	0	0	7	1	1	2	0	35
Fundamentals of Fraud	0	0	11	4	11	12	10	1	3	2	54
Information Technology Conference	43	11	35	5	7	33	1	13	7	4	159
Information Technology Symposium	0	0	0	0	0	0	0	0	0	0	0
Instructor Training School	31	1	0	0	3	3	9	3	0	0	50
International Banking School	15	5	12	0	0	2	0	0	0	1	35
International Banking (Self-study)	2	3	9	0	0	6	2	0	1	3	26
Payments Systems Risk Conference	30	4	30	7	12	21	6	0	2	2	114
Real Estate Appraisal Review School II	20	16	34	0	4	19	0	2	0	0	95
Real Estate Appraisal Review I (On-line)	5	0	24	0	2	0	0	0	1	0	32
Supervisory Updates & Emerging Issues	84	29	152	15	10	49	9	12	8	0	368
Structured Finance: Investment Analysis & Risk Management	29	5	52	0	9	8	0	2	6	0	111
Testifying School	1	0	15	0	2	10	2	0	0	1	31
Grand Total	648	245	1,391	213	167	487	48	68	52	33	3,352
Percentage	19.33	7.31	41.50	6.35	4.98	14.53	1.43	2.03	1.55	0.98	100
Combined Agency and Sponsored Percentage	26.64	NA	47.85	NA	4.98	14.53	1.43	2.03	1.55	0.98	100

Task Force on Examiner Education meeting.

Supervision's Information Technology (IT) Subcommittee and the Bank Secrecy Act/Anti-Money Laundering (BSA/AML) Working Group.

In 2012, the EEO staff, in conjunction with the IT Subcommittee, continued to coordinate revisions to the IT Examination Handbook InfoBase. Additionally, the EEO staff, in conjunction with the BSA/AML Working Group, continued to update the BSA/AML Examination Manual InfoBase.

Facilities

The FFIEC rents office space, classrooms, and lodging facilities at the Federal Deposit Insurance Corporation's Seidman Center in Arlington, Virginia. This facility offers convenient access to two auditoriums and numerous classrooms.

topics, to review feedback from each course and conference, and to develop a framework for future courses and conferences. The solid partnership between the task force principals and the EEO staff promotes open and regular communication that continues to result in high quality, well-received training.

The EEO administered 95 sessions of courses and conferences during 2012. The total number of attendees at these task force sponsored training sessions equaled 3,352 (see table on the previous page for details of participation by program and agency).

A fourth Senior Program Administrator was added to the staff to assist with the increased training demands from the agencies and states. Also during 2012, the EEO, in collaboration with the Task Force on Consumer Compliance, planned the Consumer Compliance Specialists Conference, designed to provide continuing education to examiners with advanced consumer compliance examination experience. The

Conference was rescheduled, due to Hurricane Sandy, from October 2012 to January 2013 and a second session is planned for October 2013.

The Task Force on Examiner Education approves the development and maintenance of the InfoBase product. The InfoBase content is created and updated by members of the Task Force on

Course Catalogue and Schedule

The course catalogue and schedule are available online at www.ffiec.gov/exam/education.htm.

Cyber Crime Trends Panel during FFIEC's Financial Crimes Seminar at the FDIC's Virginia Square Hove Auditorium.

To obtain a copy, contact:

Karen K. Smith, Manager
FFIEC Examiner Education Office
3501 Fairfax Drive
Room B-3030
Arlington, VA 22226-3550

Phone: (703) 516-5588

Task Force on Information Sharing

The Task Force on Information Sharing promotes the sharing of electronic information among the Council member agencies in support of the supervision, regulation, and deposit insurance responsibilities of financial institution regulators. The task force provides a forum for Council member agencies to discuss and address issues affecting the quality, consistency, efficiency, and security of interagency information sharing. Significant matters are referred, with recommendations, to the Council for action, and the task force has delegated authority from the Council to take certain actions.

To the extent possible, the agencies build on each other's information databases to minimize duplication of effort and promote consistency. The agencies participate in a program to share, in accordance with agency policy, electronic versions of their reports of examination, inspection reports, and other communications with financial institutions. The agencies also provide each other with access to their organizations' structure, as well as financial and supervisory information on their regulated entities. The task force and its working groups use a collaborative website to share information among the Council member agencies. The task force maintains a "Data Exchange Summary" listing the data files exchanged among the

Task Force on Information Sharing meeting.

Council member agencies and a repository of communications and documents critical to information sharing.

The task force has established three working groups to address technology development issues, to perform interagency reconciliation of financial institution structure data, and to develop interagency identity management. In addition, the task force receives demonstrations and reports on agency, financial industry, and other Council initiatives pertaining to technology development (including the production and development status of the interagency Central Data Repository).

Initiatives Addressed in 2012

Technology Issues

The mission of the task force is to identify and implement technologies to make the sharing of interagency data more efficient and to accommodate changes in agency databases and technologies. The task force's Technology Working Group (TWG) meets monthly to

develop technological solutions that enhance data sharing and to coordinate the automated transfer of data files between the Council agencies. The group tracks weekly developments to provide timely resolutions of data exchange issues.

The TWG continues to develop necessary links and processes to exchange electronic documents, develop an inventory of future technology projects, and upload information to the collaborative website where documents and critical materials pertaining to interagency information exchanges are stored.

Structure Data Reconciliation

The task force's Structure Data Reconciliation Working Group (SDRWG) continued to reconcile structure data about financial institutions regulated by Council agencies to ensure that the information the agencies report is consistent and accurate. The SDRWG's quarterly reconcilements have greatly resolved structure data discrepancies among the agencies.

Identity Management

The Identity Management Working Group continued with its efforts to begin developing an Identity Management technology framework within the Council agencies. These continuing efforts are based on a 2010 white paper developed and presented to the agencies' Chief Information Officers. This document discussed the new information challenges presented by the recent financial reforms and sought a consensus on the scope and urgency of the efforts needed to meet these challenges going forward.

Coordination with Other Interagency Information Sharing Entities

In 2012, the task force continued to coordinate with new interagency information sharing entities including the Financial Stability Oversight Council (FSOC) and the Office of Financial Research (OFR). These coordination efforts enable the task force to keep apprised of new and emerging issues and to monitor progress on initiatives such as the Global Legal Entity Identifier initiative.

Interagency Loan Data Report

The task force created an interagency working group to review and enhance the interagency loan data report (ILDR) pursuant to a Conference of State Bank Supervisors inquiry in April 2011. The ILDR Working Group first met in July 2011. The ILDR guidance from 2002 lists 82 possible fields in the ILDR. Of those, five fields were required to be provided with an ILDR submission. The ILDR Working Group recognized that the highest supervisory value could be achieved by receiving data more consistently in the ILDR. As a result, in 2012, the ILDR Working Group recommended that 25 additional fields be required in the ILDR. The working group is currently seeking final approvals of communications to banks from the member agencies.

Task Force on Reports

The law establishing the Council and defining its functions requires the Council to develop uniform reporting systems for federally supervised financial institutions and their holding companies and subsidiaries. To meet this objective, the Council established the Task Force on Reports. The task force helps to develop interagency uniformity in the reporting of periodic information that is needed for effective supervision and other public policy purposes. As a consequence, the task force is concerned with issues such as the review and implementation of proposed revisions to reporting requirements; the development and interpretation of reporting instructions, including responding to inquiries about the instructions from reporting institutions and the public; the application of accounting standards to specific transactions; the development and application of processing standards; the monitoring of data quality; and the assessment of reporting burden. In addition, the task force works with other organizations, including the Securities and Exchange Commission, the Financial Accounting Standards Board, and the American Institute of Certified Public Accountants. The task force is also responsible for any special projects related to these subjects that the Council may assign.

To help the task force carry out its responsibilities, working groups are organized as needed to handle specialized or technical accounting, reporting, instructional, and processing matters. In this regard, the task force has established a Central Data Repository (CDR) Steering Committee to make business decisions needed to ensure the continued success of the CDR system, monitor its ongoing performance, and report on its status. The CDR is a secure, shared database for collecting, managing, validating, and distributing data reported in the quarterly Consolidated Reports of Condition and Income (Call Report) filed by insured banks and savings associations. The CDR also processes and distributes the Uniform Bank Performance Report (UBPR) under the oversight of the Task Force on Surveillance Systems.

Initiatives Addressed in 2012

Reporting Requirements for the Consolidated Reports of Condition and Income

The task force continued to conduct monthly interagency conference calls during 2012 to discuss Call Report instructional matters and related accounting issues to reach uniform interagency positions on these issues.

Thrift Financial Report (TFR)-to-Call Report Migration

Effective March 31, 2012, all savings associations migrated from filing the TFR to filing the Call Report. During the latter half of 2011, savings associations received information to assist them in converting to the Call Report and establishing an account with the CDR for the submission of Call Report data. The first quarter 2012 Call Report Supplemental Instructions included a separate section for savings associations, addressing aspects of the Call Report that differ from the TFR.

2012 Call Report Revisions

After receiving approval under the Paperwork Reduction Act

Task Force on Reports meeting.

(PRA) from the U.S. Office of Management and Budget (OMB), the Federal Deposit Insurance Corporation (FDIC), the Board of Governors of the Federal Reserve System (FRB), and the Office of the Comptroller of the Currency (OCC) (collectively, the banking agencies) implemented a limited number of revisions to the Call Report in March and June 2012. The revisions had initially been issued for public comment in November 2011. Two reporting changes were made in March 2012 in connection with the initial filing of the Call Report by savings associations: new items for reporting on Qualified Thrift Lender compliance and revisions to certain items used to calculate the leverage capital ratio denominator. Instructional revisions in March 2012 included guidance on the accounting and reporting treatment for capital contributions in the form of cash or notes receivable. Reporting changes that took effect in June 2012 included new items for mortgage loan representation and warranty reserves as well as past due

and nonaccrual purchased credit-impaired loans. Several new items to meet deposit insurance assessment needs, for which approval had been received from OMB in connection with a substantial revision of the Call Report assessment data schedule that took place in 2011, also were added to the Call Report in June 2012. These additional assessment items apply only to large and highly complex institutions and institutions owning another insured depository institution.

2013 Call Report Revisions

The banking agencies' November 2011 Call Report proposal also contained new schedules for the collection of disaggregated loan loss allowance data and selected loan origination data from larger institutions, which generated substantive comments. After modifying the proposed loan loss allowance schedule in response to comments received, the task force approved the addition of this new schedule to the Call Report effec-

tive March 31, 2013. This schedule, which OMB approved in January 2013, will be applicable to institutions with $1 billion or more in total assets. Although the agencies considered alternative approaches to collecting loan origination data in an effort to address industry comments on the proposal, the task force decided not to pursue implementation of this proposed new schedule in the Call Report. Institutions were notified of these decisions in the fourth quarter of 2012.

In the second quarter of 2012, the task force began evaluating several recommendations from the banking agencies and the Consumer Financial Protection Bureau (CFPB) for potential Call Report revisions to be implemented in 2013. As it considered these potential reporting changes, the task force also sought to limit the extent to which the changes would apply to community institutions. In the fourth quarter, the task force agreed to include several revisions in a proposal to be issued for comment. The proposed Call Report revisions, which generally would take effect in June 2013, include consumer deposit account balance data, details on service charges on consumer deposit accounts, information about and data on international remittance transfers, depository institution trade names used on physical branches and Internet Web sites that differ from an institution's legal title, the total liabilities of an institution's parent depository institution holding company that is not a bank or savings and loan holding company, and a scope revision to an existing item in the equity capital reconciliation. The proposal would also contain new and revised items for use in the FDIC's deposit insurance pricing model for large and highly complex institutions as well as instructional revisions to implement October 2012 definitional amendments to this model in the FDIC's assessment regulations, supplemented by a tabular presentation of two-year default probabilities by type of consumer loan. The proposed collection of consumer deposit account balances and pricing model data would apply to institutions with $1 billion or more and $10 billion or more in total assets, respectively. Publication of an initial PRA Federal Register notice seeking comment for 60 days on these proposed Call Report revisions is expected in February 2013.

Statutory Review of the Call Report

Under the auspices of the task force, staff from the banking agencies, the CFPB, and State Liaison Committee completed a review of "the information and schedules that are required to be filed by an insured depository institution" in the Call Report, which was mandated by section 604 of the Financial Services Regulatory Relief Act of 2006. The task force surveyed 153 users representing diverse groups within the banking agencies, the CFPB, and state supervisory authorities to identify the purposes for which each group uses each reported data item, the extent of usage for each item, and the frequency with which each item is needed. The survey was completed in September and the results were evaluated by an interagency working group that presented its findings to the task force, which reported on the results of the review to the FFIEC principals in November 2012. Section 604 also requires that, after completing the review of the reports, the banking agencies are to reduce or eliminate the continued collection of information that they determine is "no longer necessary or appropriate." In 2013, the task force will consider the

information received from survey respondents on the usage of the data in the Call Report to determine where possible burden-reducing revisions may be made.

Central Data Repository

During 2012, the banking agencies continued to devote significant staff resources to enhance the CDR for the processing of the quarterly Call Report, production of the UBPR, and the public data distribution (PDD) of those data. Savings associations were successfully transitioned into the CDR during the March 2012 Call Report processing cycle.

In September 2012, the banking agencies implemented a major CDR enhancement release. The September release included UBPR processing improvements, security enhancements, and UBPR integration with the new FDIC Examination Tools Suite.

In preparation for the expiration of the current CDR contract on November 30, 2013, an interagency procurement working group was formed to author the Statement of Work and Request for Proposal (RFP). On October 31, 2012 the Council approved proceeding with a solicitation for services to support Call Report and UBPR processing under a new CDR contract. The RFP was then issued to approved vendors. The new CDR contract is expected to be awarded by April 2013.

Other Activities

In June 2012, the banking agencies requested comment on three notices of proposed rulemaking that would revise and replace their current regulatory capital standards. The banking agencies also adopted a joint final rule revising their market risk capital rules in June 2012. Accordingly,

banking agency subject matter experts met periodically during 2012 to discuss and begin developing potential revisions to the Call Report's regulatory capital schedule and the Advanced Capital Adequacy Framework Regulatory Reporting Requirements (FFIEC 101 report) as well as possible new market risk reporting requirements. These efforts will continue under the task force's auspices during 2013.

In June 2012, the banking agencies requested comment on three notices of proposed rulemaking that would revise and replace their current regulatory capital standards. The banking agencies also adopted a joint final rule revising their market risk capital rules in June 2012. Banking agency subject matter experts met periodically during 2012 to discuss and begin developing potential revisions to the Call Report's regulatory capital schedule and the Advanced Capital Adequacy Framework Regulatory Reporting Requirements (FFIEC 101 report) as well as possible new market risk reporting requirements. These efforts will continue under the task force's auspices during 2013.

During the recent financial crisis, the banking agencies found that the level of detail provided in the current version of the Country Exposure Report (FFIEC 009 report) was insufficient to capture the evolving risks from U.S. institutions' foreign exposures. Beginning in the second quarter of 2012, banking agency subject matter experts developed recommended enhancements to increase the usefulness of this report and the related publicly available Country Exposure Information Report (FFIEC 009a report) for policy makers, bank supervisors, and market participants. In broad terms, the proposed revisions to the FFIEC 009 report would increase the number of counterparty categories, add information on the type of claims being reported, provide detail on a limited number of risk mitigants, add more detailed reporting of credit derivatives, add the United States as a country for which exposures are reported, and expand the reporting panel to include savings and loan holding companies. The FFIEC 009a report would be expanded to include additional information for those individual countries for which the disclosure threshold is triggered. Publication of an initial PRA Federal Register notice seeking comment for 60 days on these proposed reporting revisions is expected in January 2013. Subject to the comments received, the revisions to the FFIEC 009 and 009a reports would take effect June 30, 2013.

Task Force on Supervision

The Task Force on Supervision coordinates and oversees matters relating to safety-and-soundness supervision and examination of depository institutions. It provides a forum for Council members to promote quality, consistency, and effectiveness in examination and other supervisory practices. While significant issues are referred, with recommendations, to the Council for action, the Council has delegated to the task force the authority to make certain decisions and recommendations, provided all task force members agree. Meetings are held regularly to address and resolve common supervisory issues. The task force has also established and maintains supervisory communication protocols to be used in emergencies. These protocols are periodically tested through exercises with task force members and key supervisory personnel.

Task Force on Supervision meeting.

The task force has one subcommittee and one permanent working group:

- *The Information Technology (IT) Subcommittee* serves as a forum to address information systems and technology policy issues as they relate to financial institutions and their technology service providers (TSPs). The IT Subcommittee develops and maintains the FFIEC Information Technology Examination Handbook, which consists of a series of topical booklets addressing issues such as information security. Through the FFIEC, the federal banking agencies coordinate the interagency Multi-Regional Data Processing Servicer (MDPS) examination and Shared Application Software Review (SASR) programs. Through the MDPS program, the agencies conduct joint IT examinations of the largest and most complex TSPs that provide critical data processing and related banking services to regulated financial institutions. The SASR program

provides a mechanism for the agencies to review and share information on mission-critical software applications, such as loans, deposits, credit, BSA/ AML, general ledger systems and other critical software tools that are used by financial institutions. These programs help the agencies identify potential systemic risks and provide examiners with information that can reduce the time and resources needed to examine IT-related processing operations, software, and outsourced services at user financial institutions. In conjunction with the Task Force on Examiner Education, the IT Subcommittee sponsors an annual Information Technology Conference for examiners.

- *The Bank Secrecy Act/Anti-Money Laundering (BSA/ AML) Working Group* seeks to enhance coordination of BSA/ AML training, guidance, and policy. Working group coordination includes ongoing communication between federal and state banking agencies and the Financial Crimes Enforcement Network. The BSA/AML Working Group also meets periodically with other federal agencies, including the Internal Revenue Service, Securities and Exchange Commission, U.S. Commodity Futures Trading Commission, Treasury Department's Office of Terrorist Financing and Financial Crimes, and the Office of Foreign Assets Control. The BSA/AML Working Group builds on existing practices and works to strengthen the activities that are already being pursued by other formal and informal interagency groups providing oversight of various BSA/AML matters. BSA/AML training, guidance, and policy include (1) procedures and resource materials for examination purposes, (2) joint examiner training related to the FFIEC's BSA/AML Examination Manual, (3) outreach to the banking industry on BSA/AML policy matters, and (4) other issues related to consistency of BSA/AML supervision.

The task force also establishes ad hoc working groups to handle individual projects and assignments, as needed.

Initiatives Addressed in 2012

Interest Rate Risk Management

While some degree of interest rate risk is inherent in the business of banking, institutions are expected to have sound risk-management practices in place for monitoring, measuring, and where necessary, mitigating their exposure to interest rate risk. On January 12, 2012, the FFIEC released a "frequently asked questions" (FAQs) document in response to questions and

to promote the consistent application of the *2010 Interagency Advisory on Interest Rate Risk Management*. The advisory and FAQs, which were adopted by the federal banking agencies, the NCUA, and the SLC, address practices essential to effective risk management, including stress test assumption development that reflects the institution's experience, and comprehensive model validation. The FAQs reaffirm supervisory expectations for institutions to manage interest rate risk exposures using processes and systems commensurate with their complexity, business models, risk profile, and scope of operations.

Stress Testing by Community Banks

In response to questions from the task force, the FRB, FDIC, and OCC prepared a document entitled *Statement to Clarify Supervisory Expectations for Community Banks*, which was issued jointly on May 14, 2012. The Statement addresses the agencies' supervisory expectation that all banking organizations, regardless of size, should have the capacity to analyze the potential impact of adverse outcomes on their financial condition. It also reaffirms that community banks are not required or expected to conduct the types of stress testing specifically articulated in agencies' rules and guidance to implement Dodd-Frank Act requirements directed at larger organizations.

Financial Institutions Affected by Drought Conditions

To assist financial institutions and borrowers in areas affected by severe drought conditions, the Council published a *Statement on the Impact of Drought Conditions on Financial Institutions* on October 16, 2012. The statement encourages institutions to work constructively with borrowers and to consider

alternatives for prudently restructuring credit facilities as appropriate. The effects of natural disasters on the agricultural industry are often transitory, and prudent loan modification efforts can help stabilize borrowers, benefit the long-term interests of financial institutions and their stakeholders, and contribute to the health of local economies.

Charter Conversions/Dodd-Frank Restrictions

On November 26, 2012, the FRB, the FDIC, and the OCC, in conjunction with the Conference of State Bank Supervisors, published an *Interagency Statement on Section 612 of the Dodd-Frank Act: Restrictions on Conversions of Troubled Banks*. An interagency group developed the guidance, which explains the requirements of section 612 and the processes through which certain banks or savings associations should apply to convert their charters. Insured depository institutions should consider the statement in connection with the *2009 FFIEC Statement on Regulatory Conversions*, which covers a broader range of circumstances than section 612 and remains in effect.

Information Technology

Financial institutions' significant use of information technology services, whether generated internally or obtained from third-party service providers, contributes to their operational risk environment in general and their data security risk in particular. A major effort of the IT Subcommittee and agencies is maintaining the *FFIEC Information Technology Examination Handbook* (IT Handbook) and providing guidance to the industry and the agencies' field examiners on emerging IT issues and risks. The IT Handbook is updated and maintained electronically using the FFIEC InfoBase vehicle. During the year, certain enhancements were made to the IT Handbook InfoBase, including the addition of a "What's New" function on the home page that may be used to monitor recent changes and, going forward, to access a historical listing of changes. A new "Reference Materials" section also was added.

On October 31, 2012, the FFIEC published an update of the *Supervision of Technology Service Providers Booklet* of the IT Handbook. Concurrently, the FRB, FDIC, and OCC issued new *Administrative Guidelines for the Implementation of the Interagency Program for the Supervision of Technology Service Providers*. The booklet contains guidance for examiners and financial institutions on the supervision of third-party technology service providers (TSPs). It also outlines the Risk-Based Examination Priority Ranking Program and includes an appendix describing the Uniform Rating System for Information Technology, which the agencies use for financial institutions and their TSPs. Although closely related to the booklet, the guidelines are not part of the IT Handbook.

In response to a growing number of financial institutions outsourcing all or part of their security management function, the IT Subcommittee issued guidance entitled *Managed Security Service Providers*. The guidance is in the form of an appendix to the *Outsourcing Technology Service Providers Booklet*. The new appendix addresses the risks associated with Managed Security Service Providers engagement and offers guidance to assist institutions in mitigating the risks.

On July 10, 2012, the FFIEC issued guidance entitled *Outsourced Cloud Computing*. The FFIEC member agencies consider cloud comput-ing to be another form of outsourcing with the same basic risk characteristics and risk-management requirements as traditional forms of outsourcing. The guidance addresses key risk considerations associated with outsourced cloud computing activities and identifies applicable risk mitigation considerations contained in the various booklets that comprise the IT Handbook.

BSA/AML Working Group

The BSA/AML Working Group is responsible for maintaining and providing timely updates to the BSA/AML Examination Manual. The working group sponsored its sixth FFIEC Advanced BSA/AML Specialists Conference in July 2012. Feedback from the conference was positive. The agencies continued to share information with the Financial Crimes Enforcement Network and with the Office of Foreign Assets Control.

Task Force on Surveillance Systems

The Task Force on Surveillance Systems oversees the development and implementation of uniform interagency surveillance and monitoring systems. It provides a forum for the member agencies to discuss best practices to be used in those systems and to consider the development of new financial analysis tools. The task force's principal objective has been to develop and produce the Uniform Bank Performance Report (UBPR). UBPRs present financial data and peer group statistics of individual financial institutions for current and historical periods. These reports are important tools for completing supervisory evaluations of a financial institution's condition and performance, as well as for planning onsite examinations. The banking agencies also use the data from these reports in their automated monitoring systems to identify potential or emerging problems in insured financial institutions.

A UBPR is produced for each insured bank and savings association in the United States that is supervised by the FRB, FDIC, or OCC. UBPR data are also available to all state bank supervisors. While the UBPR is principally designed to meet the examination and surveillance needs of the federal and state banking agencies, the task force also makes the UBPR available to financial institutions and the public through a public website, www.ffiec.gov/UBPR.htm.

Initiatives Addressed in 2012

Thrift Financial Report Consolidation into Call Report

When the Dodd-Frank Act dissolved OTS, OCC and FDIC mandated that thrift institutions formerly regulated by OTS begin filing Call Reports no later than March 31, 2012. The task force determined that all thrift institutions will be placed into the existing FDIC-insured savings bank asset-based peer groups. There are currently four FDIC-insured savings bank peer groups: insured savings banks having assets less than $100 million, insured savings banks having assets between $100 million and $300 million, insured savings banks having assets between $300 million and $1 billion, and insured savings banks having assets greater than $1 billion. As of March 31, 2012, thrift institutions were placed in the existing FDIC-insured savings bank asset-based peer groups.

The task force agreed to create supplementary peer groups based on savings banks' owner-

Task Force on Surveillance Systems meeting.

UBPR Fiduciary and Related Services pages were completed. The updated pages now provide users with a more complete view of an institution's fiduciary activities.

Enhancements to UBPR Ratio Documentation

In 2011, the task force explored different options for presenting technical data to explain UBPR ratios. The task force agreed to develop an online UBPR technical reference manual as well as an electronic version in PDF format. In September 2012, the task force completed an online UBPR User's Guide, which is based on the CDR system taxonomy. Concurrently, the task force completed a rewrite of the companion PDF UBPR User's Guide, which was re-focused as a technical reference manual with much of its content derived from the online UBPR User's Guide. The UBPR User's Guide has long been a critical supplement to the UBPR. With the new online version, users are provided real-time access to all ratio calculations and detailed information on components of each element. The online format significantly improves the accessibility to updated calculations when elements are changed.

UBPR Delivered to a Wide Audience

UBPRs for December 31, 2011; March 31, 2012; June 30, 2012; and September 30, 2012, were produced and delivered during 2012 to federal and state banking agencies. Additionally, the UBPR website was utilized to deliver the same data to financial institutions and the general public. The task force strives to deliver the most up-to-date UBPR data to all users. Thus, current and historic UBPR data is updated nightly. Frequent updating allows the UBPR to remain synchronized with new

ship status: mutually owned or stock-owned. The newly created supplemental savings bank peer groups provide pre-defined customized peer groups that many examiners should find useful. When generating a UBPR for a savings bank or thrift institution, users will have the option to select the standard savings bank asset-based peer group or the new supplemental savings bank peer group based on the institution's ownership structure, either mutually owned or stock-owned. The asset-based savings bank peer group remains the default selection when a UBPR is generated for any thrift institution or savings bank. The new supplemental savings bank peer groups were implemented in September 2012.

Enhancements to Liquidity and Funding Ratios

In 2010, the task force approved a working group to review UBPR treatment of liquidity measures and overall funding analysis.

In 2011, the working group concluded its review and agreed on the metrics to be modified, added, or deleted. Modifications were made based on perspectives of a broad group of users, resulting in a significantly improved UBPR page. Analytical elements were added to take full advantage of newly collected data. The task force approved the working group's recommendations. In September 2012, the enhancements to the UBPR liquidity and funding metrics were completed.

Enhancements to Fiduciary Activities Ratios

In 2010, the task force approved a working group to review UBPR treatment of fiduciary data obtained from Call Report Schedule RC-T. In 2011, the working group concluded its review and agreed on the metrics to be modified, added, or deleted. The task force approved the working group's recommendations. In September 2012, the enhancements to

Call Report data as it is being submitted by financial institutions.

Other Activities

- *Content Working Group*—The task force has agreed to establish a UBPR working group to perform a complete review of the UBPR (excluding the fiduciary data activities and liquidity pages that were reviewed in 2010 and 2011) and make recommendations for potential enhancements.

- *Technology Working Group*—The task force has agreed to establish a UBPR working group to look at ways to improve the usability of the UBPR. For example, the development of various visualization options (i.e. graphs, charts) and the creation of a mobile application will be explored.

- *Supplementary Analysis Working Group*—The task force has agreed to establish a UBPR working group to identify other analytics (besides the UBPR) that could be developed and maintained under the purview of the task force.

- *Review of the online and PDF UBPR User's Guide*—The new online UBPR User's Guide and related PDF UBPR User's Guide are based on the existing CDR system taxonomy. Because the taxonomy is very extensive, consisting of thousands of UBPR and Call Report concepts, the task force agreed to review the taxonomy to ensure the accuracy and consistency of all UBPR concepts (which includes descriptions, narratives, and formulas), contained in both the online and PDF UBPR User's Guide.

Information Available on the UBPR Website

UBPR Availability

To provide broad industry and public access to information about the financial condition of insured financial institutions, the task force publishes UBPR data for each institution shortly after the underlying Call Report is filed in the CDR. The UBPR is frequently refreshed to reflect amendments to underlying Call Report data and to incorporate any content-based changes agreed to by the task force. The online UBPR is a dynamic report that is closely synchronized with the underlying Call Report.

Other UBPR Reports

Several web-based statistical reports supporting UBPR analysis are also available and are updated nightly on the website. These reports (1) summarize the performance of all UBPR peer groups (determined by size, location, and business line), (2) detail the distribution of UBPR performance ratios for financial institutions in each of these peer groups, (3) list the individual financial institutions included in each peer group, and (4) compare a financial institution to the performance of a user-defined custom peer group.

Custom Peer Group Tool

The Custom Peer Group Tool allows industry professionals, regulators, and the general public to create custom peer groups based on financial and geographical criteria. The tool can then display all UBPR pages with peer group statistics and percentile rankings derived from the custom peer group. The Custom Peer Group Tool can re-compute the entire UBPR using a custom peer group of up to 2,000 financial institutions and deliver the results usually within seconds.

Bulk Data Download

The UBPR database within the CDR containing all data appearing on report pages for all financial institutions may be downloaded as either a delimited file or in XBRL format. The service is free, and downloads are typically fast.

Please visit www.ffiec.gov/UBPR.htm for additional information about the UBPR, including status, descriptions of pending changes, and the UBPR Users Guide. The site also provides access to the reports described above. For questions about the UBPR, contact support by calling 1-888-237-3111, e-mailing cdr.help@ffiec.gov, or writing the Council at:

FFIEC
3501 Fairfax Drive, Room B7081a
Arlington, VA 22226-3550

The Federal Financial Institution Regulatory Agencies and Their Supervised Institutions

The FRB, FDIC, OCC, and NCUA have primary federal supervisory jurisdiction over 14,189 domestically chartered banks, savings associations, and federally insured credit unions. On December 31, 2012, these financial institutions held total assets of just over $17.6 trillion. The FRB has primary federal supervisory responsibility for commercial bank holding companies (BHCs) and, as of July 21, 2011, for savings and loan holding companies (SLHCs).

Three banking agencies on the Council have authority to oversee the operations of U.S. branches and agencies of foreign banks. The International Banking Act of 1978 (IBA) authorizes the OCC to license federal branches and agencies of foreign banks and permits U.S. branches that accept only whole-sale deposits to apply for insurance with the FDIC. According to the Federal Deposit Insurance Corporation Improvement Act of 1991 (FDICIA), foreign banks that wish to operate insured entities in the United States and accept retail deposits must organize under separate U.S. charters. Existing insured retail branches may continue to operate as branches. The IBA also subjects those U.S. offices of foreign banks to many provisions of the Federal Reserve Act and the Bank Holding Company Act. The IBA gives primary examining authority to the OCC, FDIC, and various state authorities for the offices within their jurisdictions. The IBA also gives the FRB residual examining authority over all U.S. banking operations of foreign banks. The Dodd-Frank Act provides statutory authority to the CFPB to conduct examinations of insured depository entities with total assets over $10 billion and their affiliates (in addition to certain nonbank entities) to ensure consumer financial products and services conform to certain federal consumer financial laws.

Board of Governors of the Federal Reserve System

The Federal Reserve Board (FRB) was established in 1913. It is headed by a seven-member Board of Governors; each member is appointed by the President, with the advice and consent of the Senate, for a 14-year term. Subject to confirmation by the Senate, the President selects one Board member to serve a four-year term as Chairperson and two members to serve as Vice Chairs; one serves in the absence of the Chairperson and the other is designated as Vice Chair for Supervision. The Chairperson also serves as a voting member of the Financial Stability Oversight Council. One member of the Board of Governors serves as the Board's representative to the FFIEC. The FRB's activities most relevant to the work of the Council are the following:

- overseeing the quality and efficiency of the examination and supervision function of the 12 Federal Reserve Banks;

- developing, issuing, implementing, and communicating regulations, supervisory policies, and guidance, and taking appropriate enforcement actions applicable to those organizations that are within the FRB's supervisory oversight authority;

- approving or denying applications for mergers, acquisitions, and changes in control by state member banks and BHCs (including financial holding companies (FHCs)); applications for foreign operations of member banks and Edge Act and agreement corporations; and applications by foreign banks to establish or acquire U.S. banks and to establish U.S. branches, agencies, or representative offices; and

- supervising and regulating:

  — State member banks (i.e., state-chartered banks that are members of the Federal Reserve System);

  — BHCs, including FHCs;

  — SLHCs;[1]

  — Edge Act and agreement corporations; select nonbank financial firms;

  — International operations of banking organizations headquartered in the United States and the domestic activities of foreign banking organizations, in conjunction with the responsible licensing authorities; as well as,

  — Nonbank financial firms designated as systemically important by the Financial Stability Oversight Council (FSOC).

Other supervisory and regulatory responsibilities of the FRB include monitoring compliance by entities under the Board's jurisdiction with other statutes (e.g., the money-laundering provisions of the Bank Secrecy Act), monitoring compliance with certain statutes that protect consumers in credit and deposit transactions, regulating margin requirements on securities transactions, and regulating transactions between banking affiliates.

---

1. The FRB's role as supervisor of BHCs, FHCs, and SLHCs is to review and assess the consolidated organization's operations, risk-management systems, and capital adequacy to ensure that the holding company and its nonbank subsidiaries do not threaten the viability of the company's depository institutions. In this role, the FRB serves as the "umbrella supervisor" of the consolidated organization. In fulfilling this role, the FRB relies, to the fullest extent possible, on information and analysis provided by the appropriate supervisory authority of the company's bank, securities, or insurance subsidiaries.

Policy decisions are implemented by the FRB or under delegated authority to the Director for the Division of Banking Supervision and Regulation, the Director for the Division of Consumer and Community Affairs, and to the 12 Federal Reserve Banks—each of which has operational responsibility within a specific geographical area. The Reserve Bank Districts are headquartered in Boston, New York, Philadelphia, Cleveland, Richmond, Atlanta, Chicago, St. Louis, Minneapolis, Kansas City, Dallas, and San Francisco. Each Reserve Bank has a president (chief executive officer) who serves for five years and is appointed by the Reserve Bank's class B and class C directors, and other executive officers who report directly to the president. Among other responsibilities, a Reserve Bank employs a staff of examiners who examine state member banks and Edge Act and agreement corporations, conduct BHC inspections, and examine the international operations of foreign banks—whose head offices are usually located within the Reserve Bank's District. When appropriate, examiners also visit the overseas offices of U.S. banking organizations to obtain financial and operating information to evaluate adherence to safe and sound banking practices.

National banks, which must be members of the Federal Reserve System, are chartered, regulated, and supervised by the OCC. State-chartered banks may apply to and be accepted for membership in the Federal Reserve System, after which they are subject to the supervision and regulation of the FRB, which is coordinated with the state's banking authority. Insured state-chartered banks that are not members of the Federal Reserve System are regulated and supervised by the FDIC. The FRB also has overall responsibility for foreign banking operations, including both U.S. banks operating abroad and foreign banks operating branches within the United States.

The Dodd-Frank Act directs the FRB to collect assessments, fees, and other charges that are equal to the expenses incurred by the Federal Reserve to carry out its responsibilities with respect to supervision of (1) BHCs and SLHCs with assets equal to or greater than $50 billion and (2) all nonbank financial companies supervised by the FRB.

Additionally, the Dodd-Frank Act created an independent CFPB within the Federal Reserve System.

The FRB covers the expenses of the CFPB's operations with revenue it generates principally from assessments on the 12 Federal Reserve Banks.

Consumer Financial
Protection Bureau

Consumer Financial Protection Bureau

The Consumer Financial Protection Bureau (CFPB) was created in 2010 by the Dodd-Frank Act and assumed transferred authorities from other federal agencies, and other new authorities, on July 21, 2011. The CFPB is an independent agency and is funded principally by transfers from the FRB up to a limit set forth in the statute. The CFPB requests transfers from the Board in amounts that are reasonably necessary to carry out its mission. Funding is capped at a preset percentage of the total 2009 operating expenses of the Federal Reserve System, subject to an annual adjustment. The Director of the CFPB serves on the FDIC Board of Directors and the Financial Stability Oversight Council.

The CFPB seeks to foster a consumer financial marketplace where customers can clearly see prices and risks up front and can easily make product comparisons; in which no one can build a business model around unfair, deceptive, or abusive practices; and that works for American consumers, responsible providers, and the economy as a whole. To accomplish this, the CFPB works to help consumer financial markets operate by making rules more effective, by consistently and fairly enforcing those rules, and by empowering consumers to take more control over their economic lives.

The Dodd-Frank Act sets forth the following functions for the CFPB:

- conducting financial education programs;

- collecting, investigating, and responding to consumer complaints;

- collecting, researching, monitoring, and publishing information relevant to the identification of risks to consumers and the proper functioning of financial markets;

- issuing rules, orders, and guidance implementing federal consumer financial laws;

- taking appropriate enforcement action to address violations of federal consumer financial laws; and

- supervising covered entities to assess compliance with federal consumer financial laws and detect financial risks to consumers.

The CFPB has statutory authority to conduct examinations to ensure that consumer financial products and services conform to certain federal consumer financial laws, and for related purposes. The CFPB's supervision program oversees:

- Insured depository entities with total assets over $10 billion and their affiliates. These institutions collectively hold more than 80 percent of the banking industry's assets.

- Certain nondepository entities regardless of size—mortgage companies (originators, brokers, and servicers, as well as related loan modification or foreclosure relief services firms), payday lenders, and private education lenders. The CFPB can also supervise the larger players, or "larger participants," as defined by rule, in consumer financial markets, and certain nondepository entities that it determines are posing a risk to consumers in connection with the offering or provision of consumer financial products or services. In 2012, the CFPB began identifying other markets in which it will supervise the larger participants and published final rules that allow it to supervise larger participants in the

— consumer reporting market (these entities have more than $7 million in annual receipts resulting from consumer reporting) and

— consumer debt collection market (these entities have annual receipts of more than $10 million resulting from consumer debt collection).

The CFPB's supervisory activities are conducted by the Division of Supervision, Enforcement, Fair Lending and Equal Opportunity. The division is headquartered in Washington, D.C., with regional offices in San Francisco (West), Chicago (Midwest), New York (Northeast), and Washington, D.C. (Southeast). Examination staff is assigned to one of the four regions.

Federal Deposit Insurance Corporation

Congress created the Federal Deposit Insurance Corporation (FDIC or Corporation) in 1933 to promote stability and public confidence in our nation's banking system. The FDIC accomplishes its mission by insuring deposits, examining and supervising financial institutions for safety and soundness and consumer protection, and managing receiverships. In its unique role as deposit insurer, the FDIC works in cooperation with other federal and state regulatory agencies to identify, monitor, and address risks to the Deposit Insurance Fund (DIF) posed by insured depository institutions.

Management of the FDIC is vested in a five-member Board of Directors. No more than three board members may be of the same political party. Three of the directors are appointed by the President, with the advice and consent of the Senate, for six-year terms. One of the three appointed directors is designated by the President as Chairman for a five-year term and another is designated as Vice Chairman. The other two board members are the Comptroller of the Currency and the Director of the CFPB. The Chairman also serves as a member of the Financial Stability Oversight Council.

Operational Structure

The FDIC's operations are organized into three major program areas: insurance, supervision, and receivership management. A description of each of these areas follows:

Insurance: The FDIC maintains stability and public confidence in the U.S. financial system by providing deposit insurance. As insurer, the

Corporation must continually evaluate and effectively manage how changes in the economy, financial markets, and banking system affect the adequacy and viability of the DIF. When an insured depository institution fails, the FDIC ensures that the financial institution's customers have timely access to their insured deposits and other services.

The FDIC provides the public with a sound deposit insurance system by supplying comprehensive statistical information on banking; identifying and analyzing emerging risks; conducting research that supports deposit insurance, banking policy, and risk assessment; assessing the adequacy of the DIF; and maintaining an effective and fair risk-based premium system.

The Dodd-Frank Act revised the statutory authorities governing the FDIC's management of the DIF. As a result, the FDIC developed a comprehensive, long-range management plan for the DIF to reduce pro-cyclicality in the deposit insurance system and maintain a positive fund balance even during a banking crisis. The plan sets an appropriate target fund size and a strategy for assessment rates and dividends. Pursuant to the comprehensive plan, the FDIC adopted a Restoration Plan to ensure that the reserve ratio reaches the statutory mandates required by the Dodd-Frank Act in a timely manner. Also pursuant to the Dodd-Frank Act, the FDIC amended its regulations to define the assessment base as average consolidated total assets minus average tangible equity, rather than domestic deposits (which, with minor adjustments, it has been since 1935).

The FDIC also continued its efforts to improve risk differentiation by issuing a rule that revised the assessment system applicable to large insured depository institutions to (1) better reflect risk in a timely manner, (2) differentiate large institutions during periods of good economic conditions, and (3) take into account the losses that the FDIC may incur if such an institution fails.

Supervision: The FDIC has primary federal regulatory and supervisory authority over insured state-chartered banks that are not members of the Federal Reserve System and for state-chartered savings associations. As deposit insurer, the FDIC also has backup examination and enforcement authority over all insured institutions. Accordingly, the FDIC can examine for insurance purposes any insured financial institution, either directly or in cooperation with state or other federal supervisory authorities. The FDIC can also recommend that the appropriate federal banking agency take action against an insured institution and may do so itself if it deems necessary. The Dodd-Frank Act also authorizes the FDIC to manage the failure of systemically significant firms.

The FDIC's supervisory activities for risk management and consumer protection are primarily organized into two divisions, the Division of Risk Management Supervision (RMS) and the Division of Depositor and Consumer Protection (DCP). RMS oversees the safety and soundness of FDIC-supervised institutions. DCP oversees the FDIC's consumer protection functions, including its examination and enforcement programs for FDIC-supervised institutions with assets of $10 billion or less. Under the Dodd-Frank Act, the FDIC retains examination and enforcement authority for several laws and regulations, including the Community

Reinvestment Act, without regard to the size of an institution.

These two divisions are further organized into six regional offices located in Atlanta, Chicago, Dallas, Kansas City, New York, and San Francisco; and two area offices located in Boston (reports to New York) and Memphis (reports to Dallas). In addition to the regional and area offices, the FDIC maintains 86 field offices for risk management and 76 field offices for compliance, with dedicated examiners assigned to many of the largest financial institutions.

Receivership Management: Bank resolutions are handled by the Division of Resolutions and Receiverships. In protecting insured deposits, the FDIC is charged with resolving failed depository institutions at the least possible cost to the DIF. In carrying out this responsibility, the FDIC engages in several activities, including paying off depositors, arranging the purchase of assets and assumption of liabilities of failed institutions, effecting insured deposit transfers between institutions, creating and operating temporary bridge banks until a resolution can be accomplished, and using its conservatorship powers.

Also, the Dodd-Frank Act vests the FDIC with authority to resolve a failing systemically important financial company, including a bank holding company, if use of that authority would avoid or mitigate potential adverse consequences for the financial system, and complies with other statutory standards. Consistent with these responsibilities, as well as its role on the FSOC helping to promote

financial stability, the FDIC has backup examination authority to include certain bank holding companies and systemically- important financial companies designated by the FSOC for supervision by the FRB.

The Division of Resolutions and Receiverships maintains personnel in its field office in Dallas and its temporary satellite office in Jacksonville, Florida; it also maintains staff in each of the FDIC regional and area offices.

Office of Complex Financial Institutions

The Office of Complex Financial Institutions (OCFI) is an organization within the FDIC created to provide a comprehensive focus to the supervisory, insurance, and resolution risks posed by the largest and most complex financial institutions. The organization ensures the effective evaluation, analysis, management, and mitigation of risk related to large and complex financial institutions. OCFI develops strategies, metrics, and supervisory plans to ensure readiness to conduct the resolution of large and complex financial institutions, thereby reducing loss exposure to the DIF and mitigating systemic risks. OCFI defines and executes the FDIC's evolving role in the oversight of large financial firms, including the expanded responsibilities assigned the FDIC by the Dodd-Frank Act. This operational group complements and enhances the FDIC's operational activities, as they relate to systemically significant institutions.

National Credit Union Administration

The National Credit Union Administration (NCUA), established by Congress in 1970 through section 1752a of the Federal Credit Union Act, is the independent federal agency that supervises the nation's federal credit union system. A three-member bipartisan board, appointed by the President for six-year terms, manages the NCUA. The President also selects one board member to serve as the Chairman. The Chairman also serves as a member of the Financial Stability Oversight Council.

The NCUA's main responsibilities are as follows:

- charter, regulate, and supervise more than 4,200 federal credit unions in the United States and its territories;

- administer the National Credit Union Share Insurance Fund (NCUSIF), which insures member share accounts in just over 6,800 federal and state-chartered credit unions;

- administer the Temporary Corporate Credit Union Stabilization Fund, which has borrowing authority from the U.S. Treasury and assessment authority to resolve corporate credit union issues; and

- manage the Central Liquidity Facility, created to improve the financial stability of credit unions by providing liquidity to the credit union system.

The NCUA also has statutory authority to examine and supervise NCUSIF-insured, state-chartered credit unions in coordination with state regulators.

The NCUA is headquartered in Alexandria, Virginia, and has five regional offices across the United States to administer its responsibilities for chartering and supervising credit unions. Additionally, the Asset Management and Assistance Center located in Austin, Texas, manages the recovery of assets for liquidated credit unions. NCUA examiners conduct on-site examinations and supervision of each federal credit union and selected state-chartered credit unions. The NCUA is funded by the credit unions it regulates and insures.

Office of the Comptroller of the Currency

The Office of the Comptroller of the Currency (OCC) is the oldest federal bank regulatory agency, established as a bureau of the Treasury Department by the National Currency Act of 1863. It is headed by the Comptroller of the Currency, who is appointed to a five-year term by the President with the advice and consent of the Senate. The Comptroller is also a Director of the FDIC and a member of the Financial Stability Oversight Council.

The OCC was created by Congress to charter, regulate, and supervise national banks. On July 21, 2011, pursuant to the Dodd-Frank Act, the OCC assumed supervisory responsibility for federal savings associations, as well as rulemaking authority relating to all savings associations. The OCC regulates and supervises 1,338 national banks and trust companies, 573 federal savings associations, and 47 federal branches of foreign banks—accounting for approximately 71 percent of the total assets of all U.S. commercial banks, federal savings associations, and branches of foreign banks. The OCC seeks to ensure that national banks and federal savings associations (collectively "banks") safely and soundly manage their risks, comply with applicable laws, compete effectively with other providers of financial services, offer products and services that meet the needs of customers, and provide fair access to financial services and fair treatment of their customers.

The OCC's mission-critical programs include:

- chartering banks and issuing interpretations related to permissible banking activities;

- establishing and communicating regulations, policies, and operating guidance applicable to banks; and

- supervising the national system of banks and savings associations through on-site examinations, off-site monitoring, systemic risk analyses, and appropriate enforcement activities.

To meet its objectives, the OCC maintains a nationwide staff of bank examiners and other professional and support personnel. Headquartered in Washington, DC, the OCC has four district offices, which are located in Chicago, Dallas, Denver, and New York. In addition, the OCC maintains a network of 73 field offices and 20 satellite locations in cities throughout the United States, as well as resident examiner teams in 23 of the largest national banking companies and an examining office in London, England.

The Comptroller receives advice on policy and operational issues from an Executive Committee comprised of senior agency officials who lead major business units.

The OCC is funded primarily by semiannual assessments on banks, interest revenue from its investment in U.S. Treasury securities, and other fees. The OCC does not receive congressional appropriations for any of its operations.

ASSETS, LIABILITIES, AND NET WORTH of U.S. Commercial Banks, Savings Institutions, and Credit Unions as of December 31, 2012[1]

Billions of dollars

Item	Total	U.S. Commercial Banks[2]			U.S. Branches and Agencies of Foreign Banks[6]	Savings Institutions[4]		Credit Unions[3]	
		National	State Member[5]	State Non-Member		OCC Regulated Federal Charter	FDIC Regulated State Charter[7]	Federal Charter	State Charter
Total assets	*17,613*	*9,271*	*2,005*	*2,122*	*2,134*	*719*	*340*	*557*	*465*
Total loans and receivables (net)	8,639	4,627	909	1,358	519	414	217	322	273
Loans secured by real estate[8]	4,444	2,277	506	830	31	289	191	168	152
Consumer loans[9]	1,604	919	70	246		87	6	156	120
Commercial and industrial loans	1,778	988	224	232	273	35	20	2	4
All other loans and lease receivables[10]	984	554	125	76	215	10	3	–	1
LESS: Allowance for loan and lease losses	170	111	16	25		7	3	4	4
Federal funds sold and securities purchased under agreements to resell	729	500	30	16	180	1	1	–	1
Cash and due from depository institutions[11]	2,256	801	358	177	674	64	29	80	73
Securities and other obligations[12]	3,402	1,858	478	415	165	192	67	131	96
U.S. government obligations[13]	745	242	77	87	60	27	53	115	84
Obligations of state and local governments[14]	263	125	46	80		6	6	–	–
Other securities	2,394	1,491	355	248	105	159	8	16	12
Other assets[15]	2,586	1,485	231	155	595	48	26	24	22
Total liabilities	*15,872*	*8,240*	*1,781*	*1,868*	*2,134*	*634*	*299*	*499*	*417*
Total deposits and shares[16]	12,702	6,766	1,588	1,659	1,008	545	258	475	403
Federal funds purchased and securities sold under agreements to repurchase	783	340	56	31	327	20	9	–	
Other borrowings[17]	1,201	623	63	145	261	55	28	18	8
Other liabilities[18]	1,185	511	73	33	538	14	4	6	6
Net worth[19]	*1,742*	*1,031*	*224*	*254*	*1*	*85*	*41*	*58*	*48*
Memorandum: Number of institutions reporting	14,189	1,294	843	4,018	228	547	440	4,272	2,547

Footnotes to Tables

1. The table covers institutions, including those in Puerto Rico and U.S. territories and possessions, insured by the Federal Deposit Insurance Corporation or National Credit Union Savings Insurance Fund. All branches and agencies of foreign banks in the United States, but excluding any in Puerto Rico and U.S. territories and possessions, are covered whether or not insured. Excludes Edge Act and agreement corporations that are not subsidiaries of U.S. commercial banks.

2. Reflects fully consolidated statements of FDIC-insured U.S. commercial banks—including their foreign branches, foreign subsidiaries, branches in Puerto Rico and U.S. territories and possessions, and FDIC insured banks in Puerto Rico and U.S. territories and possessions. Excludes bank holding companies.

3. Data are for federally insured natural person credit unions only.

4. Reflects fully consolidated statements of Savings Institutions—including Stock Savings Banks, Mutual Savings Banks, Stock Savings & Loan Associations, and Mutual Savings & Loan Associations that are Federally Chartered or that are State Chartered and not Federal Reserve Members.

5. Includes State Member Savings Banks and State Member Cooperative Banks.

6. These institutions are not required to file reports of income.

7. Includes State Chartered Savings Associations formerly regulated by the Office of Thrift Supervision.

8. Includes loans secured by residential property, commercial property, farm-land (including improvements) and unimproved land; and construction loans secured by real estate.

9. Includes loans, except those secured by real estate, to individuals for household, family, and other personal expenditures including both installment and single payment loans. Net of unearned income on installment loans.

10. Includes loans to financial institutions, for purchasing or carrying securities, to finance agricultural production and other loans to farmers (except those secured by real estate), to states and political subdivisions and public authorities, and miscellaneous types of loans.

Notes continue on the next page

INCOME AND EXPENSES of U.S. Commercial Banks, Savings Institutions, and Credit Unions for the Twelve Months Ending December 31, 2012[1]

Billions of dollars

Item	Total	U.S. Commercial Banks[2]			Savings Institutions[4]		Credit Unions[3]	
		National	State Member[5]	State Non-Member	OCC Regulated Federal Charter	FDIC Regulated State Charter[7]	Federal Charter	State Charter
Operating income:	768	469	90	118	48	15	28	23
Interest and fees on loans	404	233	40	79	25	10	17	14
Other interest and dividend income	103	69	13	11	5	2	3	2
All other operating income	261	167	37	28	18	3	8	7
Operating expenses:	570	348	66	86	35	12	23	19
Salaries and benefits	194	120	27	28	7	4	8	7
Interest on deposits and shares	47	22	5	10	4	2	4	3
Interest on other borrowed money	25	15	2	4	2	1	1	
Provision for loan and lease losses	61	39	4	10	5	1	2	2
All other operating expenses	244	152	28	35	17	4	8	7
Net operating income	*198*	*121*	*24*	*32*	*13*	*3*	*5*	*4*
Securities gains and losses	8	6	1	1				
Extraordinary items								
Income taxes	58	37	7	8	5	1	–	–
Net income	*147*	*90*	*18*	*24*	*8*	*2*	*5*	*4*
Memorandum: Number of institutions reporting	13,961	1,294	843	4,018	547	440	4,272	2,547

11. Includes vault cash, cash items in process of collection, and balances with U.S. and foreign banks and other depository institutions (including demand and time deposits and certificates of deposit for all categories of institutions).

12. Includes government and corporate securities, including mortgage-backed securities and obligations of states and political subdivisions and of U.S. government agencies and corporations.

13. U.S. Treasury securities and securities of, and loans to, U.S. government agencies and corporations.

14. Securities issued by states and political subdivisions and public authorities, except for U.S. branches and agencies of foreign banks that do not report these securities separately. Loans to states and political subdivisions and

public authorities are included in "All other loans and lease receivables."

15. Customers liabilities on acceptances, real property owned, various accrual accounts, and miscellaneous assets. For U.S. branches and agencies of foreign banks, also includes net due from head office and other related institutions.

16. Includes demand, savings, and time deposits, (including certificates of deposit at commercial banks, U.S. branches and agencies of foreign banks, and savings banks), credit balances at U.S. agencies of foreign banks and share balances at credit unions (including certificates of deposit, NOW accounts, and share draft accounts). For U.S. commercial banks, includes deposits in foreign offices, branches in U.S. territories and possessions, and Edge Act and Agreement corporation subsidiaries.

17. Includes interest-bearing demand notes issued to the U.S. Treasury, borrowing from Federal Reserve Banks and Federal Home Loan Banks, subordinated debt, limited life preferred stock, and other nondeposit borrowing.

18. Includes depository institutions own mortgage borrowing, liability for capitalized leases, liability on acceptances executed, various accrual accounts, and miscellaneous liabilities. For U.S. branches and agencies of foreign banks, also includes net owed to head office and other related institutions.

19. Includes capital stock, surplus, capital reserves, and undivided profits.

NOTE: Data are rounded to nearest billion. Consequently some information may not reconcile precisely. Additionally, balances less than $500 million will show as zero.

Appendix A: Relevant Statutes

Federal Financial Institutions Examination Council Act

12 U.S.C. § 3301. *Declaration of purpose*

It is the purpose of this chapter to establish a Financial Institutions Examination Council which shall prescribe uniform principles and standards for the Federal examination of financial institutions by the Office of the Comptroller of the Currency, the Federal Deposit Insurance Corporation, the Board of Governors of the Federal Reserve System, the Federal Home Loan Bank Board, and the National Credit Union Administration and make recommendations to promote uniformity in the supervision of these financial institutions. The Council's actions shall be designed to promote consistency in such examination and to insure progressive and vigilant supervision.

12 U.S.C. § 3302. *Definitions*

As used in this chapter—

(1) the term "Federal financial institutions regulatory agencies" means the Office of the Comptroller of the Currency, the Board of Governors of the Federal Reserve System, the Federal Deposit Insurance Corporation, the Office of Thrift Supervision, and the National Credit Union Administration;

(2) the term "Council" means the Financial Institutions Examination Council; and

(3) the term "financial institution" means a commercial bank, a savings bank, a trust company, a savings association, a building and loan association, a homestead association, a cooperative bank, or a credit union.

12 U.S.C. § 3303. *Financial Institutions Examination Council*

(a) Establishment; composition

There is established the Financial Institutions Examination Council which shall consist of—

(1) the Comptroller of the Currency,

(2) the Chairman of the Board of Directors of the Federal Deposit Insurance Corporation,

(3) a Governor of the Board of Governors of the Federal Reserve System designated by the Chairman of the Board,

(4) the ***Director of the Consumer Financial Protection Bureau,***[1]

(5) the Chairman of the National Credit Union Administration Board; and

(6) the Chairman of the State Liaison Committee

(b) Chairmanship

The members of the Council shall select the first chairman of the Council. Thereafter the chairmanship shall rotate among the members of the Council.

(c) Term of office

---

1. The Dodd Frank Wall Street Reform and Consumer Protection Act of 2010 amended several provisions in the relevant statutes, including excerpts contained in this appendix. Changes are shown as bolded and italicized. The amendments relating to the Consumer Financial Protection Bureau became effective on July 21, 2011.

The term of the Chairman of the Council shall be two years.

(d) Designation of officers and employees

The members of the Council may, from time to time, designate other officers or employees of their respective agencies to carry out their duties on the Council.

(e) Compensation and expenses

Each member of the Council shall serve without additional compensation but shall be entitled to reasonable expenses incurred while carrying out his official duties as such a member.

12 U.S.C. § 3304. *Costs and expenses of Council*

One-fifth of the costs and expenses of the Council, including the salaries of its employees, shall be paid by each of the Federal financial institutions regulatory agencies. Annual assessments for such share shall be levied by the Council based upon its projected budget for the year, and additional assessments may be made during the year, if necessary.

12 U.S.C. § 3305. *Functions of Council*

(a) Establishment of principles and standards

The Council shall establish uniform principles and standards and report forms for the examination of financial institutions which shall be applied by the Federal financial institutions regulatory agencies.

(b) Making recommendations

regarding supervisory matters and adequacy of supervisory tools

(1) The Council shall make recommendations for uniformity in other supervisory matters, such as, but not limited to, classifying loans subject to country risk, identifying financial institutions in need of special supervisory attention, and evaluating the soundness of large loans that are shared by two or more financial institutions. In addition, the Council shall make recommendations regarding the adequacy of supervisory tools for determining the impact of holding company operations on the financial institutions within the holding company and shall consider the ability of supervisory agencies to discover possible fraud or questionable and illegal payments and practices which might occur in the operation of financial institutions or their holding companies.

(2) When a recommendation of the Council is found unacceptable by one or more of the applicable Federal financial institutions regulatory agencies, the agency or agencies shall submit to the Council, within a time period specified by the Council, a written statement of the reasons the recommendation is unacceptable.

(c) Development of uniform reporting system

The Council shall develop uniform reporting systems for federally supervised financial institutions, their holding companies, and non-financial institution subsidiaries of such institutions or holding companies. The authority to develop uniform reporting systems shall not restrict or amend the requirements of section 78l(i) of Title 15.

(d) Conducting schools for examiners and assistant examiners

The Council shall conduct schools for examiners and assistant examiners employed by the Federal financial institutions regulatory agencies. Such schools shall be open to enrollment by employees of State financial institutions supervisory agencies and employees of the Federal Housing Finance Board under conditions specified by the Council.

(e) Affect on Federal regulatory agency research and development of new financial institutions supervisory agencies

Nothing in this chapter shall be construed to limit or discourage Federal regulatory agency research and development of new financial institutions supervisory methods and tools, nor to preclude the field testing of any innovation devised by any Federal regulatory agency.

(f) Annual report

Not later than April 1 of each year, the Council shall prepare an annual report covering its activities during the preceding year.

(g) Flood insurance

The Council shall consult with and assist the Federal entities for lending regulation, as such term is defined in section 4121(a) of Title 42, in developing and coordinating uniform standards and requirements for use by regulated lending institutions under the national flood insurance program.

12 U.S.C. § 3306. State liaison

To encourage the application of uniform examination principles and standards by State and Federal supervisory agencies, the Council shall establish a liaison committee composed of five representatives of State agencies which supervise financial institutions which shall meet at least twice a year with the Council. Members of the liaison com-mittee shall receive a rea-

sonable allowance for necessary expenses incurred in attending meetings.

Members of the Liaison Committee shall elect a chairperson from among the members serving on the committee.

12 U.S.C. § 3307. Administration

(a) Authority of Chairman of Council

The Chairman of the Council is authorized to carry out and to delegate the authority to carry out the internal administration of the Council, including the appointment and supervision of employees and the distribution of business among members, employees, and administrative units.

(b) Use of personnel, services, and facilities of Federal financial institutions regulatory agencies, Federal Reserve banks, and Federal Home Loan Banks.

In addition to any other authority conferred upon it by this chapter, in carrying out its functions under this chapter, the Council may utilize, with their consent and to the extent practical, the personnel, services, and facilities of the Federal financial institutions regulatory agencies, Federal Reserve banks, and Federal Home Loan Banks, with or without reimbursement therefore.

(c) Compensation, authority, and duties of officers and employees; experts and consultants

In addition, the Council may—

(1) subject to the provisions of Title 5 relating to the competitive service, classification, and General Schedule pay rates, appoint and fix the compensation of such officers and employees as are necessary to carry out the provisions of this chapter, and to prescribe the authority and duties of such officers and employees; and

(2) obtain the services of such experts and consultants as are necessary to carry out the provisions of this chapter.

12 U.S.C. § 3308. Access to books, accounts, records, etc., by Council

For the purpose of carrying out this chapter, the Council shall have access to all books, accounts, records, reports, files, memorandums, papers, things, and property belonging to or in use by Federal financial institutions regulatory agencies, including reports of examination of financial institutions or their holding companies from whatever source, together with workpapers and correspondence files related to such reports, whether or not a part of the report, and all without any deletions.

12 U.S.C. § 3309. Risk management training

(a) Seminars

The Council shall develop and administer training seminars in risk management for its employees and the employees of insured financial institutions.

(b) Study of risk management training program

Not later than end of the 1-year period beginning on August 9, 1989, the Council shall—

(1) conduct a study on the feasibility and appropriateness of establishing a formalized risk management training program designed to lead to the certification of Risk Management Analysts; and

(2) report to the Congress the results of such study.

12 U.S.C. § 3310. Establishment of Appraisal Subcommittee

There shall be within the Council a subcommittee to be known as the "Appraisal Subcommittee," which shall consist of the designees of the heads of the Federal financial institutions regulatory agencies, the Bureau of Consumer Financial Protection, and the Federal Housing Finance Agency. Each such designee shall be a person who has demonstrated knowledge and competence concerning the appraisal profession. At all times at least one member of the Appraisal Subcommittee shall have demonstrated knowledge and competence through licensure, certification, or professional designation within the appraisal profession.

12 U.S.C. § 3311. Required review of regulations

(a) In general

Not less frequently than once every 10 years, the Council and each appropriate Federal banking agency represented on the Council shall conduct a review of all regulations prescribed by the Council or by any such appropriate Federal banking agency, respectively, in order to identify outdated or otherwise unnecessary regulatory requirements imposed on insured depository institutions.

(b) Process

In conducting the review under subsection (a) of this section, the Council or the appropriate Federal banking agency shall—

(1) categorize the regulations described in subsection (a) of this section by type (such as consumer regulations, safety and soundness regulations, or such other designations as determined by the Council, or the appropriate Federal banking agency); and

(2) at regular intervals, provide notice and solicit public comment on a particular category or categories of regulations, requesting commentators to identify areas of the regulations that are outdated, unnecessary, or unduly burdensome.

(c) Complete review

The Council or the appropriate Federal banking agency shall ensure that the notice and comment period described in subsection (b)(2) of this section is conducted with respect to all regulations described in subsection (a) of this section not less frequently than once every 10 years.

(d) Regulatory response

The Council or the appropriate Federal banking agency shall—

(1) publish in the Federal Register a summary of the comments received under this section, identifying significant issues raised and providing comment on such issues; and

(2) eliminate unnecessary regulations to the extent that such action is appropriate.

(e) Report to Congress

Not later than 30 days after carrying out subsection (d)(1) of this section, the Council shall submit to the Congress a report, which shall include—

(1) a summary of any significant issues raised by public comments received by the Council and the appropriate Federal banking agencies under this section and the relative merits of such issues; and

(2) an analysis of whether the appropriate Federal banking agency involved is able to address the regulatory burdens associated with such issues by regulation, or whether such burdens must be addressed by legislative action.

Excerpts from Statute Governing Appraisal Subcommittee

12 U.S.C. § 3332. Functions of Appraisal Subcommittee

(a) In general

The Appraisal Subcommittee shall—

(1) monitor the requirements established by States—

(A) for the certification and licensing of individuals who are qualified to perform appraisals in connection with federally related transactions, including a code of professional responsibility; and

(B) for the registration and supervision of the operations and activities of an appraisal management company; and

(2) monitor the requirements established by the Federal financial institutions regulatory agencies with respect to—

(A) appraisal standards for federally related transactions under their jurisdiction, and

(B) determinations as to which federally related transactions under their jurisdiction require the services of a State certified appraiser and which require the services of a State licensed appraiser;

(3) maintain a national registry of State certified and licensed appraisers who are eligible to perform appraisals in federally related transactions; and

(4) Omitted.

(5) transmit an annual report to the Congress not later than June 15 of each year that describes the manner in which each function assigned to the Appraisal Subcommittee has been carried out during the pre-ceding year. The report shall also detail the activities of the Appraisal Subcommittee, including the results of all audits of State appraiser regulatory agencies, and provide an accounting of disapproved actions and warnings taken in the previous year, including a description of the conditions causing the disapproval and actions taken to achieve compliance.

(6) maintain a national registry of appraisal management companies that either are registered with and subject to supervision of a State appraiser certifying and licensing agency or are operating subsidiaries of a Federally regulated financial institution.

(b) Monitoring and reviewing Foundation

The Appraisal Subcommittee shall monitor and review the practices, procedures, activities, and organizational structure of the Appraisal Foundation.

12 U.S.C. § 3333. Chairperson of Appraisal Subcommittee; term of Chairperson; meetings

(a) Chairperson

The Council shall select the Chairperson of the subcommittee. The term of the Chairperson shall be two years.

(b) Meetings; quorum; voting

The Appraisal Subcommittee shall meet in public session after notice *in the Federal Register, but may close certain portions of these meetings related to personnel and review of preliminary State audit reports*, at the call of the Chairperson or a majority of its members when there is business to be conducted. A majority of members of the Appraisal Subcommittee shall constitute a quorum but 2 or more members may hold hearings. Deci-sions of the Appraisal Subcommittee shall be made by the vote of a majority of its members. *The subject matter discussed in any closed or executive session shall be described in the Federal Register notice of the meeting.*

Excerpts from Home Mortgage Disclosure Act

12 U.S.C. § 2801. Congressional findings and declaration of purpose

(a) Findings of Congress

The Congress finds that some depository institutions have sometimes contributed to the decline of certain geographic areas by their failure pursuant to their chartering responsibilities to provide adequate home financing to qualified applicants on reasonable terms and conditions.

(b) Purpose of chapter

The purpose of this chapter is to provide the citizens and public officials of the United States with sufficient information to enable them to determine whether depository institutions are filling their obligations to serve the housing needs of the communities and neighborhoods in which they are located and to assist public officials in their determination of the distribution of public sector investments in a manner designed to improve the private investment environment.

(c) Construction of chapter

Nothing in this chapter is intended to, nor shall it be construed to, encourage unsound lending practices or the allocation of credit.

* * * * *

12 U.S.C. § 2803. Maintenance of records and public disclosure

* * *

(f) Data disclosure system; operation, etc.

The Federal Financial Institutions Examination Council, in consultation with the Secretary, shall implement a system to facilitate access to data required to be disclosed under this section. Such system shall include arrangements for a central depository of data in each primary metropolitan statistical area, metropolitan statistical area, or consolidated metropolitan statistical area that is not comprised of designated primary metropolitan statistical areas. Disclosure statements shall be made available to the public for inspection and copying at such central depository of data for all depository institutions which are required to disclose information under this section (or which are exempted pursuant to section 2805(b) of this title) and which have a home office or branch office within such primary metropolitan statistical area, metropolitan statistical area, or consolidated metropolitan statistical area that is not comprised of designated primary metropolitan statistical areas.

* * * * *

12 U.S.C. § 2809. Compilation of aggregate data

(a) Commencement; scope of data and tables

Beginning with data for calendar year 1980, the Federal Financial Institutions Examination Council shall compile each year, for each primary metropolitan statistical area, metropolitan statistical area, or consolidated metropolitan statistical area that is not comprised of designated primary metropolitan statistical areas, aggregate data by census tract for all depository institutions which are required to disclose data under section 2803 of this title or which are exempt pursuant to section 2805(b) of this title. The Council shall also produce tables indicat-

ing, for each primary metropolitan statistical area, metropolitan statistical area, or consolidated metropolitan statistical area that is not comprised of designated primary metropolitan statistical areas, aggregate lending patterns for various categories of census tracts grouped according to location, age of housing stock, income level, and racial characteristics.

(b) Staff and data processing resources

The Board shall provide staff and data processing resources to the Council to enable it to carry out the provisions of subsection (a) of this section.

(c) Availability to public

The data and tables required pursuant to subsection (a) of this section shall be made available to the public no later than December 31 of the year following the calendar year on which the data is based.

Deloitte.

Deloitte & Touche LLP
555 12th St. N.W.
Washington, DC 20004-1207
USA

Tel: +1 202 879 5600
Fax: +1 202 879 5309
www.deloitte.com

INDEPENDENT AUDITORS' REPORT

To the Federal Financial Institutions Examination Council:

We have audited the accompanying financial statements of the Federal Financial Institutions Examination Council (the "Council") which are comprised of the balance sheets as of December 31, 2012 and 2011, and the related statements of operations, and cash flows for the years then ended, and the related notes to the financial statements

Management's Responsibility for the Financial Statements

The Council's management is responsible for the preparation and fair presentation of these financial statements in accordance with accounting principles generally accepted in the United States of America; this includes the design, implementation, and maintenance of internal control relevant to the preparation and fair presentation of financial statements that are free from material misstatement, whether due to fraud or error

Auditors' Responsibility

Our responsibility is to express an opinion on these financial statements based on our audits We conducted our audits of the financial statements in accordance with auditing standards generally accepted in the United States of America and in accordance with the standards applicable to financial audits contained in *Government Auditing Standards* issued by the Comptroller General of the United States Those standards require that we plan and perform the audit to obtain reasonable assurance about whether the financial statements are free from material misstatement An audit of the financial statements involves performing procedures to obtain audit evidence about the amounts and disclosures in the financial statements The procedures selected depend on the auditor's judgment, including the assessment of the risks of material misstatement of the financial statements, whether due to fraud or error In making those risk assessments, the auditor considers internal control relevant to the Council's preparation and fair presentation of the financial statements in order to design audit procedures that are appropriate in the circumstances, but not for the purpose of expressing an opinion on the effectiveness of the Council's internal control Accordingly, we express no such opinion An audit of the financial statements also includes evaluating the appropriateness of accounting policies used and the reasonableness of significant accounting estimates made by management, as well as evaluating the overall presentation of the financial statements

We believe that the audit evidence we have obtained is sufficient and appropriate to provide a basis for our audit opinion

Member of
Deloitte Touche Tohmatsu

Opinion

In our opinion, the financial statements referred to above present fairly, in all material respects, the financial position of the Council as of December 31, 2012 and 2011, and the results of its operations and its cash flows for the years then ended in accordance with accounting principles generally accepted in the United States of America

Report on Internal Control Over Financial Reporting and on Compliance Based on an Audit of Financial Statements Performed in Accordance with Government Auditing Standards

In accordance with *Government Auditing Standards*, we have also issued our report dated February 28, 2013, on our consideration of the Council's internal control over financial reporting and on our tests of its compliance with certain provisions of laws, regulations, contracts, and grant agreements and other matters The purpose of that report is to describe the scope of our testing of internal control over financial reporting and compliance and the results of that testing, and not to provide an opinion on internal control over financial reporting or on compliance That report is an integral part of an audit performed in accordance with *Government Auditing Standards* in considering the Council's internal control over financial reporting and compliance

Deloitte r Touche LLP

February 28, 2013

FEDERAL FINANCIAL INSTITUTIONS EXAMINATION COUNCIL
Balance Sheets

	As of December 31,	
	2012	2011
ASSETS		
CURRENT ASSETS		
Cash	$ 638,550	$ 543,453
Accounts receivable from member organizations	885,200	785,708
Accounts receivable from non-menbers—net	189,930	91,520
Total current assets	1,713,680	1,420,681
NONCURRENT ASSETS		
Furniture and equipment leased—net	97,929	137,625
Central Data Repository software—net	3,393,963	5,138,312
Home Mortgage Disclosure Act software—net	1,716,718	2,273,492
Total noncurrent assets	5,208,610	7,549,429
TOTAL ASSETS	$ 6,922,290	$ 8,970,110
LIABILITIES AND CUMULATIVE RESULTS OF OPERATIONS		
CURRENT LIABILITIES		
Accounts payable and accrued liabilities payable to member organizations	$ 840,720	$ 805,796
Other accounts payable and accrued liabilities	484,866	285,947
Accrued annual leave	38,880	22,971
Capital lease payable	41,040	39,376
Deferred revenue	3,950,737	3,125,930
Total current liabilities	5,356,243	4,280,020
LONG-TERM LIABILITIES		
Capital lease payable	61,786	102,825
Deferred revenue	1,159,944	4,285,874
Deferred rent	10,085	9,996
Total long-term liabilities	1,231,815	4,398,695
Total liabilities	6,588,058	8,678,715
CUMULATIVE RESULTS OF OPERATIONS	334,232	291,395
TOTAL LIABILITIES AND CUMULATIVE RESULTS OF OPERATIONS	$ 6,922,290	$ 8,970,110

See notes to financial statements.

FEDERAL FINANCIAL INSTITUTIONS EXAMINATION COUNCIL
Statements of Operations

	For the years ended December 31,	
	2012	2011
REVENUES		
Assessments on member organizations	$ 687,332	$ 687,107
Central Data Repository	5,398,279	4,936,912
Home Mortgage Disclosure Act	3,999,638	3,727,927
Tuition	3,605,056	3,246,549
Community Reinvestment Act	949,761	946,928
Uniform Bank Performance Report	396,883	351,646
Total revenues	15,036,949	13,897,069
EXPENSES		
Data processing	4,392,625	4,164,479
Professional fees	4,277,394	4,121,224
Salaries and related benefits	2,023,401	1,781,660
Depreciation	3,371,828	2,869,594
Rental of office space	264,989	264,989
Adminstration fees	261,000	281,000
Travel	277,321	242,659
Other seminar expenses	22,694	33,526
Rental and maintenance of office equipment	33,612	27,544
Office and other supplies	34,145	56,237
Printing	23,561	18,389
Postage	1,419	2,564
Miscellaneous	10,123	5,046
Total expenses	14,994,112	13,868,911
RESULTS OF OPERATIONS	42,837	28,158
CUMULATIVE RESULTS OF OPERATIONS—Beginning of year	291,395	263,237
CUMULATIVE RESULTS OF OPERATIONS—End of year	$ 334,232	$ 291,395

See notes to financial statements.

FEDERAL FINANCIAL INSTITUTIONS EXAMINATION COUNCIL
Statements of Cash Flows

	For the years ended December 31,	
	2012	2011
CASH FLOWS FROM (USED IN) OPERATING ACTIVITIES		
Results of operations	$ 42,837	$ 28,158
Adjustments to reconcile results of operations to net cash provided by operating activities:		
Depreciation	3,371,828	2,869,594
(Increase) decrease in assets:		
Accounts receivable from member organizations	(99,492)	490,542
Other accounts receivable	(98,410)	12,921
Increase (decrease) in liabilities:		
Accounts payable and accured liabilities payable to member organizations	34,924	(33,356)
Other accounts payable and accrued liabilities	113,238	(284,515)
Accrued annual leave	15,909	(4,775)
Deferred revenue (current and non-current)	(2,583,162)	(2,080,991)
Deferred rent	89	3,391
Net cash provided by operating activities	797,761	1,000,969
CASH FLOWS FROM (USED IN) INVESTING ACTIVITIES		
Capital expenditures	(660,365)	(1,169,016)
CASH FLOWS FROM (USED IN) FINANCING ACTIVITIES		
Capital lease payments	(42,299)	(35,315)
NET INCREASE (DECREASE) IN CASH	95,097	(203,362)
CASH BALANCE—Beginning of year	543,453	746,815
CASH BALANCE—End of year	$ 638,550	$ 543,453

See notes to financial statements.

Notes to Financial Statements as of and for the Years Ended December 31, 2012 and 2011

1. Organization and Purpose

The Federal Financial Institutions Examination Council (the Council) was established under Title X of the Financial Institutions Regulatory and Interest Rate Control Act of 1978. The purpose of the Council is to prescribe uniform principles and standards for the federal examination of financial institutions and to make recommendations to promote uniformity in the supervision of these financial institutions. The five agencies represented on the Council during 2012, referred to collectively as member organizations, are as follows:

- Board of Governors of the Federal Reserve System (FRB)
- Consumer Financial Protection Bureau (CFPB)
- Federal Deposit Insurance Corporation (FDIC)
- National Credit Union Administration (NCUA)
- Office of the Comptroller of the Currency (OCC)

In accordance with the Financial Services Regulatory Relief Act of 2006, a representative state regulator was added as a full voting member of the Council in October 2006.

The Council was given additional statutory responsibilities by Section 340 of the Housing and Community Development Act of 1980, Public Law 96-399. Among these responsibilities are the implementation of a system to facilitate public access to data that depository institutions must disclose under the Home Mortgage Disclosure Act of 1975 (HMDA) and the aggregation of annual HMDA data, by census tract, for each metropolitan statistical area.

On July 21, 2010, the Dodd-Frank Wall Street Reform and Consumer Protection Act of 2010 (Dodd-Frank Act) was signed into law. This legislation substituted the director of the Consumer Financial Protection Bureau for the director of the Office of Thrift Supervision (OTS) as a member of the Council effective July 21, 2011.

The Council's financial statements do not include financial data for the Council's Appraisal Subcommittee (the Subcommittee). The Subcommittee was created pursuant to Public Law 101–73, Title XI of the Financial Institutions Reform, Recovery, and Enforcement Act of 1989. Although it is a subcommittee of the Council, the Appraisal Subcommittee maintains separate financial records and administrative processes. The Council is not responsible for any debts incurred by the Appraisal Subcommittee, nor are Appraisal Subcommittee funds available for use by the Council.

2. Significant Accounting Policies

Basis of Accounting—The Council prepares its financial statements in accordance with accounting principles generally accepted in the United States (GAAP).

Revenues—Assessments are made on member organizations to fund the Council s operations based on expected cash needs. Amounts over- or under-assessed due to differences between actual and expected cash needs are presented in the "Cumulative Results of Operations" line item during the year and then may be used to offset or increase the next year's assessment. Deficits in "Cumulative Results of Operations" can be recouped in the following year's assessments.

The Council provides training seminars in the Washington, D.C. area and at locations throughout the country for member organizations and other agencies. The Council also coordinates the production and distribution of the Uniform Bank Performance Reports (UBPR) through the FDIC. Tuition and UBPR revenue are adjusted at year-end to match expenses incurred as a result of providing education classes and UBPR services. For differences between revenues and expenses, member agencies are assessed an additional amount or credited a refund based on each member's proportional cost for the Examiner Education and UBPR budget. The Council recognizes revenue from member agencies for expenses incurred related to the Community Reinvestment Act, and the Home Mortgage Disclosure Act. The Council also recognizes revenue from other agencies and mortgage insurance companies related to the Home Mortgage Disclosure Act.

Capital Assets—Furniture and equipment is recorded at cost less accumulated depreciation. Depreciation is calculated on a straight-line basis over the estimated useful lives of the assets, which range from four to ten years. Upon the sale or other disposition of a depreciable asset, the cost and related accumulated depreciation are removed and any gain or loss is recognized. The Central Data Repository (CDR) and the HMDA processing system, internally developed software projects, are recorded at cost as required by the Internal Use Software Topic of Financial Accounting Standards Board (FASB) Accounting Standards Codification (ASC).

Deferred Revenue—Deferred revenue includes cash collected and accounts receivable related to CDR and the HMDA processing system.

Deferred Rent—The lease for office and classroom space contains scheduled rent increases over the term of the lease. As required by FASB ASC 840 Topic Leases, scheduled rent increases must be considered in determining the annual rent expense to be recognized. The deferred rent represents the difference between the actual lease payments and the rent expense recognized.

Estimates—The preparation of financial statements in conformity with GAAP requires management to make estimates and assumptions that affect the reported amounts of assets and liabilities and the disclosure of contingent assets and liabilities at the date of the financial statements and the reported amounts of revenues and expenses during the reporting period. Actual results could differ from those estimates.

Allowance for Doubtful Accounts—Accounts receivable for non-members are shown net of the allowance for doubtful accounts. Accounts receivable considered uncollectible are charged against the allowance account in the year they are deemed uncollectible. The allowance for doubtful accounts is adjusted monthly, based upon a review of outstanding receivables. The allowance for doubtful accounts is $0 and $59 for 2012 and 2011, respectively.

3. Transactions with Member Organizations

	2012	2011
Accounts Receivable		
Board of Governors of the Federal Reserve System	$ 211,061	$ 132,539
Consumer Financial Protection Bureau	42,253	0
Federal Deposit Insurance Corporation	268,871	194,230
National Credit Union Administration	42,370	46,051
Office of the Comptroller of the Currency	320,695	412,888
	$ 885,200	$ 785,708
Accounts Payable and Accrued Liabilities		
Board of Governors of the Federal Reserve System	$ 545,770	$ 494,234
Consumer Financial Protection Bureau	5,397	0
Federal Deposit Insurance Corporation	161,700	175,940
National Credit Union Administration	28,470	27,080
Office of the Comptroller of the Currency	99,383	108,542
	$ 840,720	$ 805,796
Operations		
Council operating expenses reimbursed by members	$ 687,332	$ 687,107
FRB-provided administrative support	$ 261,000	$ 281,000
FRB-provided data processing	$ 4,392,625	$ 4,164,479

Notes continue on the following page.

The Council does not directly employ personnel, but rather member organizations detail personnel to support Council operations. These personnel are paid through the payroll systems of member organizations. Salaries and fringe benefits, including retirement benefit plan contributions, are reimbursed to these organizations. The Council does not have any post-retirement or post-employment benefit liabilities since Council personnel are included in the plans of the member organizations. Due to organizational changes resulting from the Dodd-Frank Act, the OCC absorbed all financial related activity of the OTS on July 21, 2011.

Member organizations are not reimbursed for the costs of personnel who serve as Council members and on the various task forces and committees of the Council. The value of these contributed services is not included in the accompanying financial statements.

4. Central Data Repository (CDR)

In 2003, the Council entered into an agreement with UNISYS to enhance the methods and systems used to collect, validate, process, and distribute Call Report information, and to store this information in CDR. CDR was placed into service in October 2005. At that time, the Council began depreciating the CDR on the straight-line basis over its estimated useful life of 63 months. In 2009, the Council reevaluated the useful life of CDR and decided to extend the estimated useful life by an additional 36 months based on enhanced functionality of the software. The Council records depreciation expenses and recognizes the same amount of revenue. The Council also pays for hosting and maintenance expenses for CDR and recognizes the associated revenue from members. In 2012, the Council had enhancements made to CDR of $1,031,009. Some of these enhancements, which affect the asset value, were paid for directly by the FDIC. This non-cash event in the amount of $282,040 is excluded from the Statement of Cash Flows.

Capital Asset CDR

	2012	2011
Beginning balance	$20,120,566	$19,371,661
Software placed in use during the year	1,031,009	748,905
Total asset	$ 21,151,575	
Less accumulated depreciation	(17,757,612)	(14,982,254)
Central Data Repository software—net	$ 3,393,963	$ 5,138,312

Accounts Payable and Accrued Liabilities Related to CDR

	2012	2011
Payable to UNISYS for the CDR project	$ 219,762	$ 216,012

CDR *Financial Activity*—The Council is funding the project by billing the three participating Council member organizations (FRB, FDIC, and OCC). Activity for the years ended December 31, 2012 and 2011, is as follows:

Deferred Revenue

	2012	2011
Beginning balance	$ 5,138,312	$ 6,708,927
Additions	1,031,009	748,906
Less revenue recognized	(2,775,358)	(2,319,521)
Ending balance	$ 3,393,963	$ 5,138,312
Current portion deferred revenue	$ 3,393,963	$ 2,569,156
Long-term deferred revenue	0	2,569,156
Total Deferred Revenue	$ 3,393,963	$ 5,138,312

Total CDR Revenue

	2012	2011
Deferred revenue recognized	$ 2,775,358	$ 2,319,521
Hosting and maintenance revenue	2,622,921	2,617,391
Total CDR Revenue	$ 5,398,279	$ 4,936,912

Depreciation

	2012	2011
Depreciation for the CDR project	$ 2,775,358	$ 2,319,521

5. Home Mortgage Disclosure Act (HMDA)

FRB provides maintenance and support for the HMDA processing system. In 2007, the Council began a rewrite of the entire HMDA processing system, which went into service in 2011. At that time the Council began depreciating the system on the straight-line basis over its estimated useful life of 60 months. The Council records depreciation expenses and recognizes the same amount of revenue each year. The Council also pays for maintenance expenses for the HMDA processing system and recognizes the associated revenue from the members and non-members. The financial activity associated with the processing system for the years ended December 31, 2012 and 2011 is as follows:

Deferred Revenue

	2012	2011
Beginning balance	$ 2,273,492	$ 2,783,868
Additions	0	0
Less revenue recognized	(556,774)	(510,376)
Ending balance	$ 1,716,718	$ 2,273,492
Current portion deferred revenue	$ 556,774	$ 556,774
Long-term deferred revenue	1,159,944	1,716,718
Total Deferred Revenue	$ 1,716,718	$ 2,273,492

Total HMDA Revenue

The Council recognized the following revenue from:

	2012	2011
Member organizations for the production and distribution of reports under the HMDA (includes the deferred revenue recognized in 2012)	$ 3,111,398	$ 2,857,085
Department of Housing and Urban Development s participation in the HMDA project	546,809	556,207
Mortgage insurance companies for HMDA-related work	341,431	314,635
Total HMDA Revenue	$ 3,999,638	$ 3,727,927

Capital asset HMDA

	2012	2011
Beginning balance	$ 2,783,868	$ 2,783,868
Total asset	$ 2,783,868	$ 2,783,868
Less accumulated depreciation	(1,067,150)	(510,376)
HMDA software—net	$ 1,716,718	$ 2,273,492

Depreciation

	2012	2011
Depreciation for the HMDA Rewrite project	$ 556,774	$ 510,376

Notes continue on the following page.

6. Operating Leases

The Council entered into an operating lease with the FDIC in January 2010 to secure office and classroom space. Minimum annual payments under the operating lease having an initial or remaining non-cancelable lease term in excess of one year at December 31, 2012 are as follows

Years ending December 31,	Amount
2013	268,292
2014	271,772
Total minimum lease payments	$ 540,064

Rental expenses under this operating lease were $264,989 and $264,989 as of December 31, 2012 and 2011, respectively.

7. Capital Leases

In December 2009 and November 2010, the Council entered into capital leases for printing equipment. Furniture and equipment includes $198,485 for the capital leases. Accumulated depreciation is $100,556 and $60,860 for 2012 and 2011, respectively. The depreciation expense for the printing equipment is $39,697 and $39,697 for 2012 and 2011, respectively. Contingent rentals for excess usage of the printing equipment amounted to $20,544 and $13,531 in 2012 and 2011, respectively.

The future minimum lease payments required under the capital leases and the present value of the net minimum lease payments as of December 31, 2012 are as follows:

Years ending December 31,	Amount
2013	5 ,089
2014	59,089
2015	31,738
Total minimum lease payments	149,916
Less amount representing maintenance	(42,733)
Net minimum lease payments	107,183
Less amount representing interest	(4,357)
Net minimum lease payments	102,826
Less current maturities of capital lease payments	(41,040)
Long-term capital lease obligations	$ 61,786

8. Subsequent Events

There were no subsequent events that require adjustments to or disclosures in the financial statements as of December 31, 2012. Subsequent events were evaluated through February 28, 2013, which is the date the financial statements were available to be issued.

Deloitte.

Deloitte & Touche LLP
555 12th St. N.W.
Washington, DC 20004-1207
USA

Tel: +1 202 879 5600
Fax: +1 202 879 5309
www.deloitte.com

INDEPENDENT AUDITORS' REPORT ON INTERNAL CONTROL OVER FINANCIAL REPORTING AND ON COMPLIANCE AND OTHER MATTERS BASED ON AN AUDIT OF FINANCIAL STATEMENTS PERFORMED IN ACCORDANCE WITH GOVERNMENT AUDITING STANDARDS

To the Federal Financial Institutions Examination Council:

We have audited, in accordance with the auditing standards generally accepted in the United States of America and the standards applicable to financial audits contained in *Government Auditing Standards* issued by the Comptroller General of the United States, the financial statements of the Federal Financial Institutions Examination Council (the "Council"), as of and for the years ended December 31, 2012 and 2011, and the related notes to the financial statements, and have issued our report thereon dated February 28, 2013

Internal Control Over Financial Reporting

In planning and performing our audit, we considered the Council's internal control over financial reporting (internal control) to determine the audit procedures that are appropriate in the circumstances for the purpose of expressing our opinion on the financial statements, but not for the purpose of expressing an opinion on the effectiveness of the Council's internal control Accordingly, we do not express an opinion on the effectiveness of the Council's internal control

A *deficiency in internal control* exists when the design or operation of a control does not allow management or employees, in the normal course of performing their assigned functions, to prevent, or detect and correct, misstatements on a timely basis A *material weakness* is a deficiency, or a combination of deficiencies, in internal control, such that there is a reasonable possibility that a material misstatement of the entity's financial statements will not be prevented, or detected and corrected on a timely basis A *significant deficiency* is a deficiency, or a combination of deficiencies, in internal control that is less severe than a material weakness, yet important enough to merit attention by those charged with governance

Our consideration of internal control was for the limited purpose described in the first paragraph of this section and was not designed to identify all deficiencies in internal control that might be material weaknesses or significant deficiencies Given these limitations, during our audit we did not identify any deficiencies in internal control that we consider to be material weaknesses However, material weaknesses may exist that have not been identified

Compliance and Other Matters

As part of obtaining reasonable assurance about whether the Council's financial statements are free of material misstatement, we performed tests of its compliance with certain provisions of laws, regulations, contracts, and grant agreements, noncompliance with which could have a direct and material effect on the determination of financial statement amounts However, providing an opinion on compliance with those provisions was not an objective of our audit, and accordingly, we do not express such an opinion The

Member of
Deloitte Touche Tohmatsu

results of our tests disclosed no instances of noncompliance or other matters that are required to be reported under *Government Auditing Standards*.

Purpose of this Report

The purpose of this report is solely to describe the scope of our testing of internal control and compliance and the results of that testing, and not to provide an opinion on the effectiveness of the entity's internal control or on compliance This report is an integral part of an audit performed in accordance with *Government Auditing Standards* in considering the Council's internal control and compliance Accordingly, this communication is not suitable for any other purpose

Deloitte r Touche LLP

February 28, 2013

APPENDIX C: MAPS OF AGENCY REGIONS AND DISTRICTS

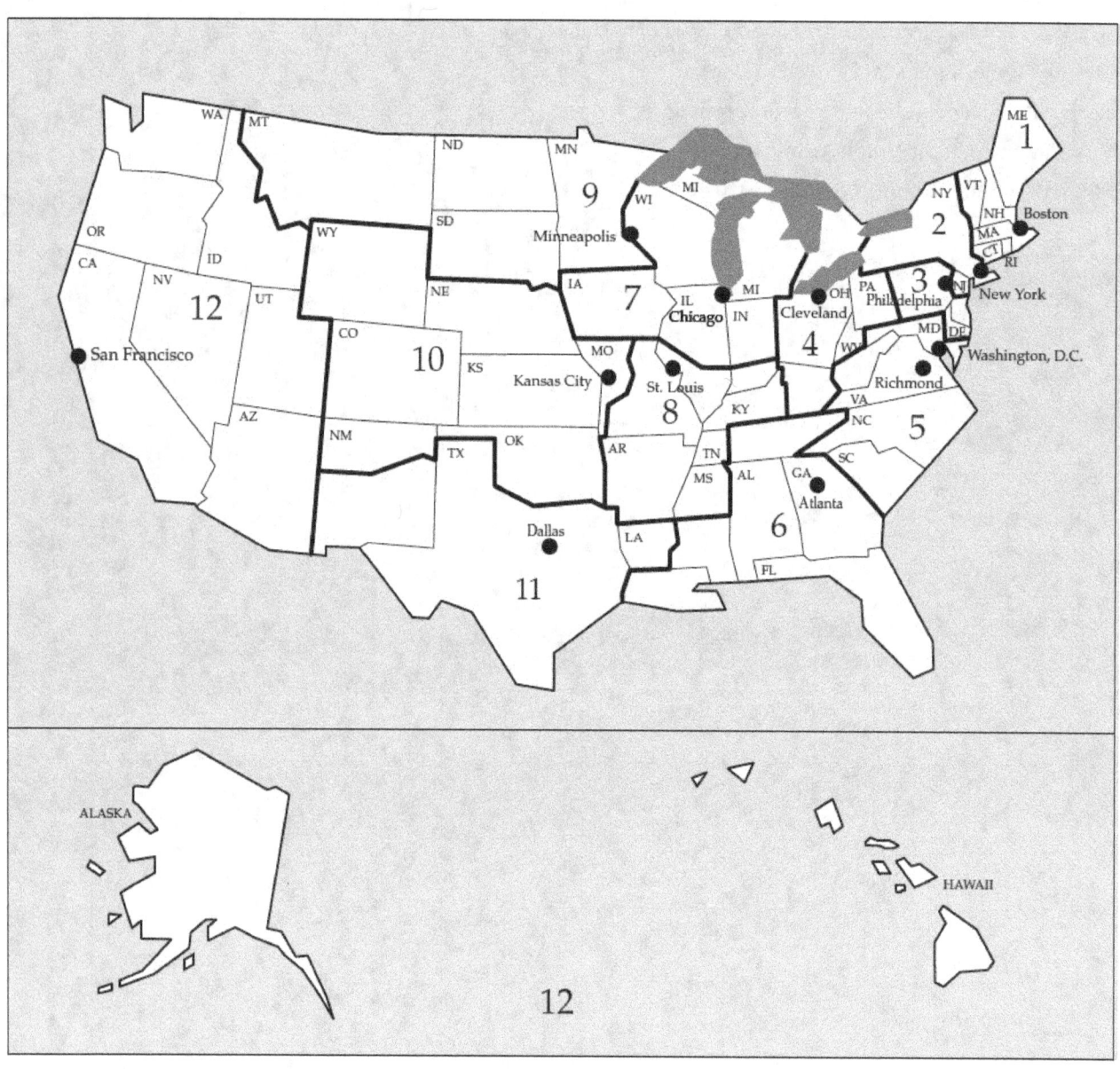

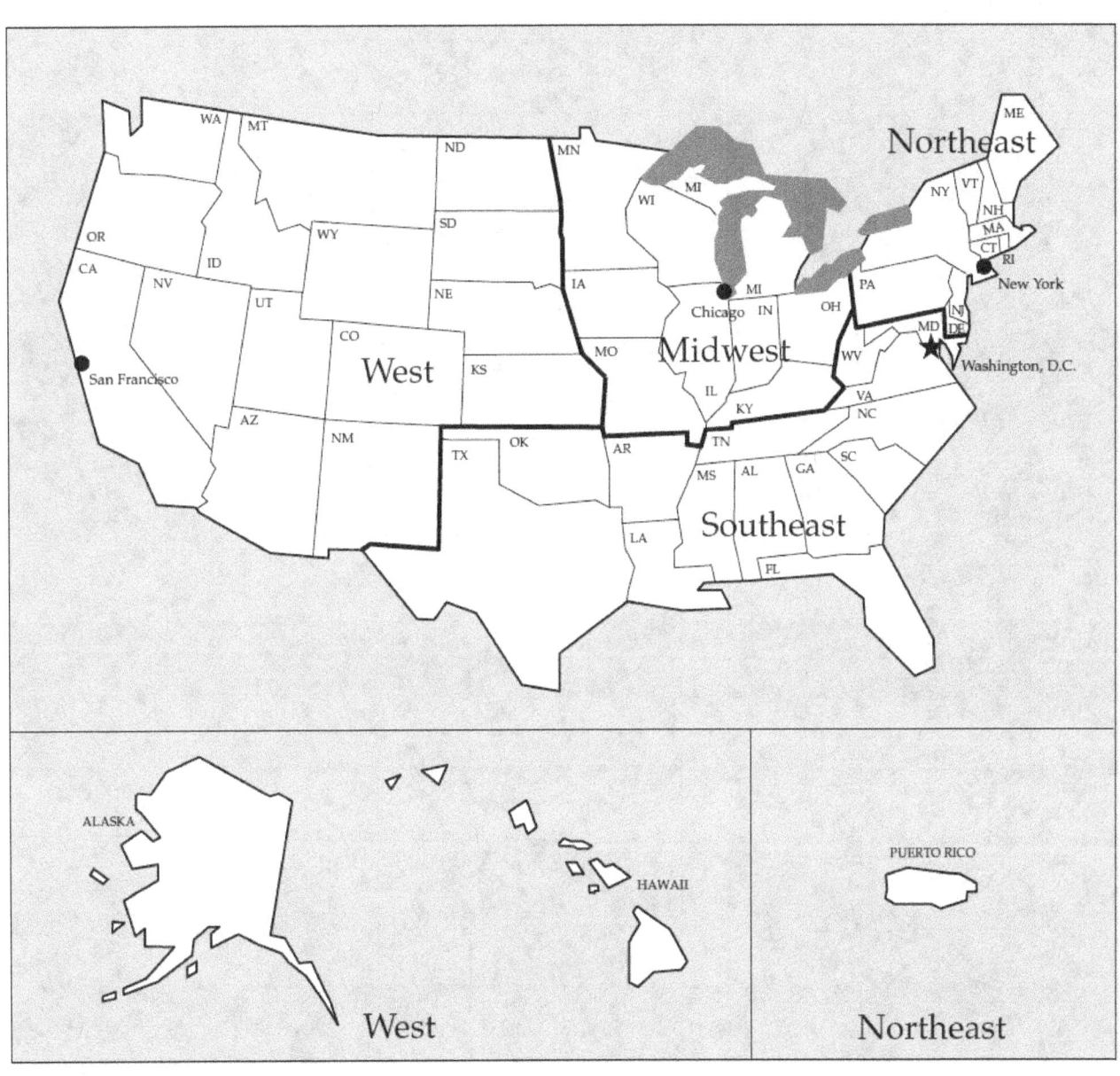

FEDERAL DEPOSIT INSURANCE CORPORATION
REGIONS (SUPERVISION AND COMPLIANCE)

* Two area offices are located in Boston
(reports to New York) and Memphis
(reports to Dallas)

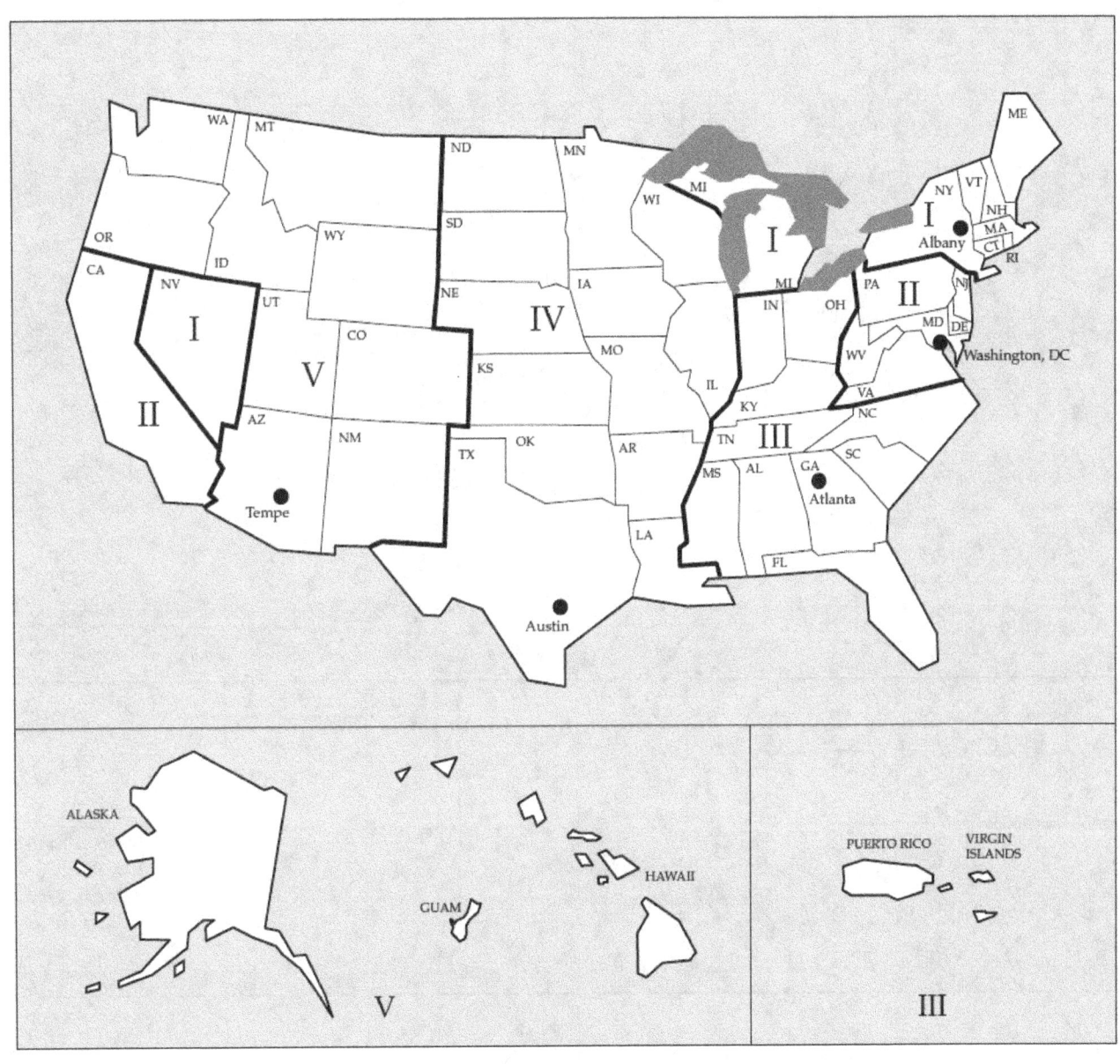

COMPTROLLER OF THE CURRENCY
DISTRICT ORGANIZATION

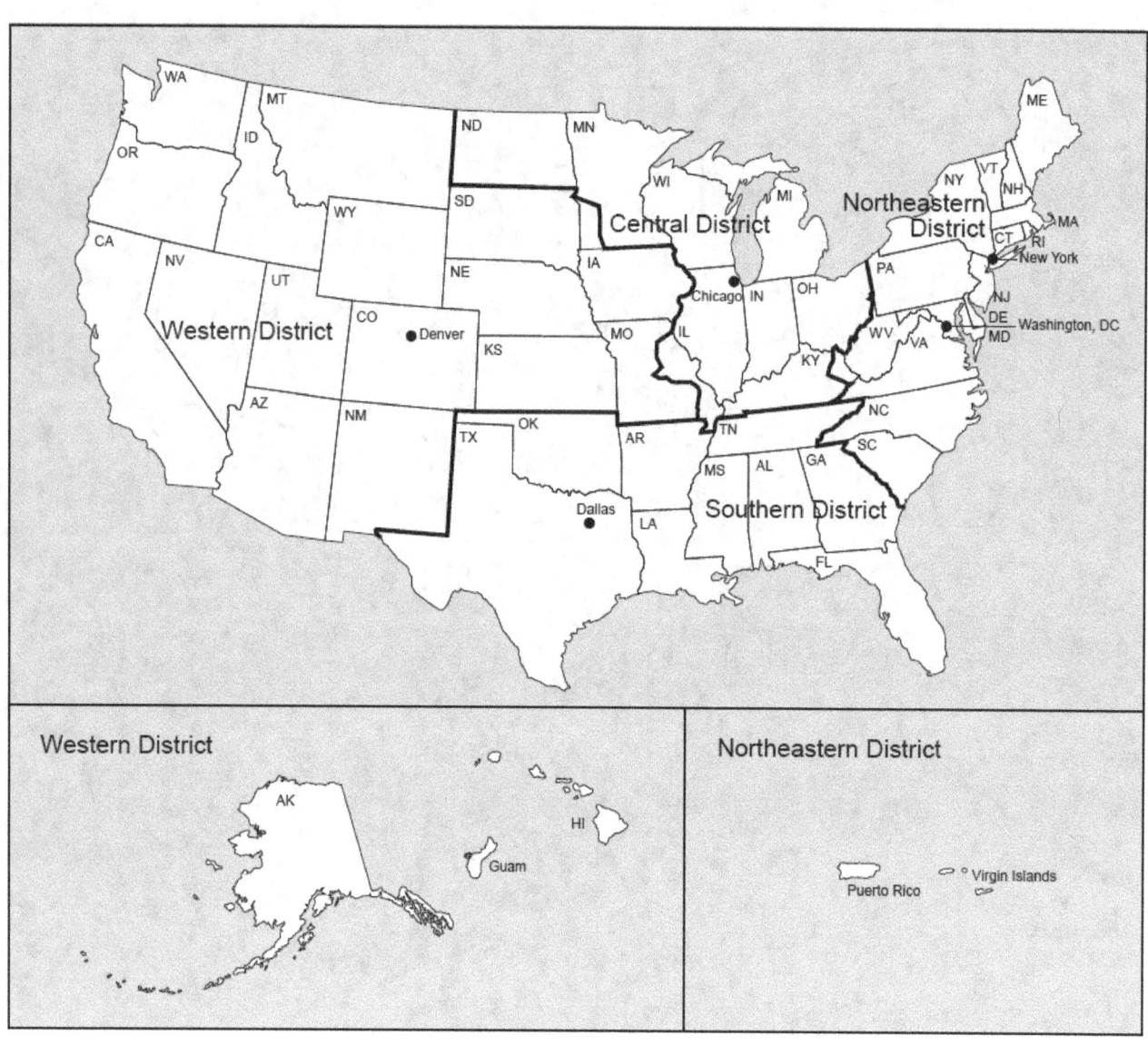

APPENDIX D: ORGANIZATIONAL LISTING OF PERSONNEL

Organization, December 31, 2012

Members of the Council

Debbie Matz, *Chairman*
  Chairman
  National Credit Union
    Administration (NCUA)

Thomas Curry, *Vice Chairman*
  Comptroller of the
    Currency
  Office of the Comptroller of the
    Currency (OCC)

Daniel K. Tarullo
  Member
  Board of Governors of the
    Federal Reserve System (FRB)

Martin J. Gruenberg
  Chairperson
  Federal Deposit Insurance
    Corporation (FDIC)

Richard Cordray
  Director
  Consumer Financial Protection
    Bureau (CFPB)

John Munn
  State Liaison Committee (SLC)
    Chairman
  Director
  Nebraska Department of
    Banking & Finance

State Liaison Committee (SLC)

John Munn, *Chairman*
  Director
  Nebraska Department of
    Banking & Finance

David Cotney
  Commissioner
  Massachusetts Division of Banks

Harold E. Feeney
  Commissioner
  Texas Credit Union Department

Douglas Foster
  Commissioner
  Texas Department of Savings
    and Mortgage Lending

Charles A. Vice
  Commissioner
  Kentucky Department of
    Financial Institutions

Council Staff Officer

Judith E. Dupre
Executive Secretary

Interagency Staff Groups

Agency Liaison Group

Larry Fazio (NCUA)
John C. Lyons (OCC)
Arthur W. Lindo (FRB)
Sandra Thompson (FDIC)
Steven Antonakes (CFPB)
Mary Beth Quist (SLC
  Representative/CSBS)

Legal Advisory Group

Michael J. McKenna, *Chairman*
  (NCUA)
Julie L. Williams (OCC),
  retired 9/12
Scott Alvarez, (FRB)
Richard J. Osterman, Jr. (FDIC)
Meredith Fuchs (CFPB)
Margaret Liu (SLC
  Representative/CSBS)

Task Force on Consumer Compliance

April Breslaw, *Chairman* (CFPB)
Luke H. Brown (FDIC)
David Cotney (SLC Member)
Carol Evans (FRB)
Grovetta N. Gardineer (OCC)
Moisette I. Green (NCUA)

Task Force on Examiner Education

Matthew J. Biliouris, *Chairman*
  (NCUA)
Norbert Cieslack (FRB)
Charlotte Corley (SLC
  Representative/Mississippi)
Mira Marshall (CFPB)
Philip D. Mento (FDIC)
Thomas E. Rollo (OCC)

Task Force on Information Sharing

Robin Stefan, *Chairman* (OCC)
John Kolhoff (SLC
  Representative, Michigan)
Michael Kraemer (FRB)
Jami Pictroski (CFPB)
Todd Roscoe (NCUA)
Terrie Templemon (FDIC)

Task Force on Reports

Robert F. Storch, *Chairman* (FDIC)
Robert T. Maahs (FRB)
LeAnn M. Meyer (SLC
  Representative/Iowa)
Kerry Morse (CFPB)
Kathy K. Murphy (OCC)
Virginia L. Phillips (NCUA)

Task Force on Supervision

John Lyons, *Chairman* (OCC)
Steven Antonakes (CFPB)
Matthew Biliouris (NCUA)
Michael S. Gibson (FRB)
Sandra Thompson (FDIC)
Charles A. Vice (SLC Member)

Task Force on Surveillance Systems

Robin Stefan, *Chairman* (OCC)
Matt Mattson (FRB)
Charles Collier (FDIC)
Abhishek Agarwal (CFPB)
Lucinda V. Johnson (NCUA)
Kyle Thomas (SLC
  Representative/CSBS)

Staff Members of the FFIEC

Shown are the FFIEC staff members at the Seidman Center in Arlington, Virginia, where they have their offices and classrooms for examiner education programs.

Federal Financial Institution Examination Council staff members (from the left to right): Michelle Clark, Ernie Larkins, Juliet Pradier, David Vallee, Cathy Pritchard, Martin Goaslind, Judith Dupre, Darlene Callis, Karen Smith, Jennifer Herring, Robert Basinger, Rosanna Piccirilli, Cynthia Curry-Daniel, and Melanie Middleton.